GARLAND
PUBLICATIONS
IN
COMPARATIVE
LITERATURE

General Editor
JAMES J. WILHELM
Rutgers University

Associate Editors
DANIEL JAVITCH, New York University
STUART Y. MCDOUGAL, University of Michigan
RICHARD SÁEZ, The College of Staten Island/CUNY
RICHARD SIEBURTH, New York University

A GARLAND SERIES

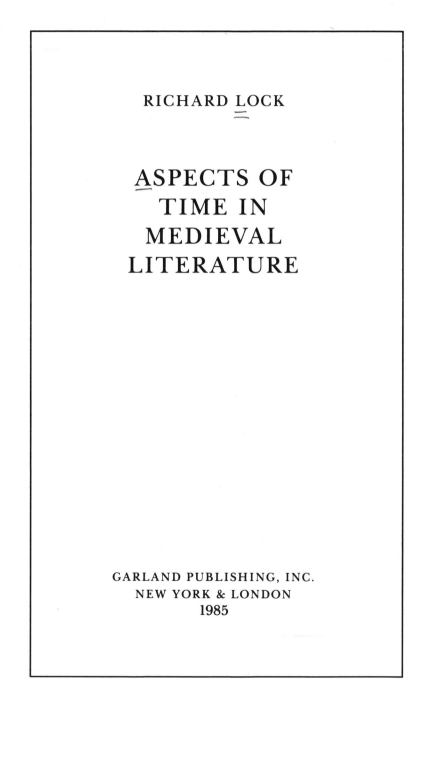

RICHARD LOCK

ASPECTS OF TIME IN MEDIEVAL LITERATURE

GARLAND PUBLISHING, INC.
NEW YORK & LONDON
1985

Library of Congress Cataloging in Publication Data

Lock, Richard, 1935–
Aspects of time in medieval literature.

(Garland publications in comparative literature)
Bibliography: p.
1. Literature, Medieval—History and criticism.
2. Time in literature.   I. Title.   II. Series.
PN682.T55L6   1985   809′.923   84-48370
ISBN 0-8240-6705-3 (alk. paper)

The volumes in this series are printed on
acid-free, 250-year-life paper.

Printed in the United States of America

ASPECTS OF TIME IN MEDIEVAL LITERATURE

Richard Lock

Quid est tempus? Si nemo quaerat, scio,
si quaerenti explicari velim, nescio.

Saint Augustine, _Confessions_, XI, 17

This dissertation is dedicated to Margaret,
without whose encouragement it would not have been possible

ABSTRACT

The aim of this investigation has been to try to develop
a new approach to the differences between oral and written
literature. Anthropological evidence indicates that concepts
of time are closely related to literacy and non-literacy.
Cyclic time is thought to be characteristic of a non-literate
society, while linear time is characteristic of a literate
group. This suggests that an examination of medieval texts
with regard to time might prove useful in refining the differences between the two catagories of literature.

Two aspects of time and their relation to narrative have
been considered. First, duration and the question of chronology: does an event occupy an appropriate quantity of time,
and does the narrative as a whole take place within a continuous and logical time-frame? Second, sequence is emphasized,
and the relation of time-sequence to the pattern of narrative
itself is discussed. Does the pattern of time, whether linear
or cyclic, dominate the narrative sequence?

Since an oral narrative belongs to a shared culture, the
story is likely to be known, thus less emphasis is placed on
expectation and more on the elaboration of "set pieces." With
a story created by a literate author, the audience may well not
know the outcome and the author can increase tension by withholding information or setting a time limit. As literacy and
a sense of history develop, time is seen as more objective,
quantitative, and less related to the natural world and the
lives of men.

The investigation produced results confirming the
relation between literacy and time concepts, and supporting
the idea of different structural patterns for oral and literary texts.

The Song of Roland has all the characteristics of an
oral narrative. Structurally, it is discontinuous and repetitive. The action moves jerkily, held up by the repetitions
which heighten emotion. There is no expectation. Time, too,
is discontinuous, being presented in a cycle of day and night
to which events are intimately linked. A chronology of events
is impossible to construct.

Yvain, Sir Gawain and the Green Knight, and "The Shipman's
Tale" are very different from the Roland. The style and narrative struture of all three works are linear and hypotactic.
Time in an important element in each plot and is used by the
authors to intensify emotion. A chronology can be discerned
for at least a major part of each work. Time has become more
objective.

Among the other texts, Atlakviða is close to the Roland.
The narrative is broken up by journeys which are outside time;
no chronology can be constructed, and the style is repetitious.
Gunnlaugs Saga is also structurally similar to the Roland, but
the crisis of the plot depends on a time-limit and the story
is clearly connected to known historical events.

In Beowulf there is a very strong feeling of linear time
both within the poem itself and in the way the audience is
distanced in time by the narrator. Nearly all the "digressions"

involve shifts in time, some of which are in the poem's future but in the audience's past. On this evidence, I should place <u>Beowulf</u> among the literary works.

Although the texts chosen are from a variety of cultures, their similarities and differences cross those boundaries. The texts closer to one end of the oral-literary spectrum have more in common than texts which share the same language. It is difficult, of course, to drawn firm conclusions. Detailed analyses of more texts must be made as well as investigations of other traditional genres such as folktales.

TABLE OF CONTENTS

I   Introduction   1

II   Accounting for Time: Early Texts   34

III   Accounting for Time: Later Texts   62

IV   Patterns of Time and Narrative: Early Texts   114

V   Patterns of Time and Narrative: Later Texts   186

       Conclusion   244

       List of Works Consulted   257

Chapter I: INTRODUCTION

Recent investigations into the differences between
oral and written literature have largely concerned the
problem of deciding what was orally composed and what was
composed originally in writing.[1] The techniques of the oral
composition of poetry have been clearly described from the
observation of living "singers of tales," and it has been
shown that a knowledge of such techniques enables a nonliterate
singer to compose and recite long poems which would be
impossible to remember word for word.[2]

Behind differences in technique, however, lie differences
which stem from fundamental contrasts between the societies
in which the oral and the literate poet live: differences of
great significance in an approach to oral literature. If the
different characteristics of oral and written literature
stemming from the societies which produce them can be made
clear, we shall be closer to developing an esthetic for oral
literature, a task which, with few exceptions, has not been
attempted.[3] In like manner, for example, Epic and Romance
are extensively compared without an attempt to discover
whether contrasts in ideals and ethics may be linked to basic
differences between the societies which produced these works.[4]

Frequently critics use criteria developed for one kind
of culture to comment on the products of a society with
completely different values and attitudes -- an Icelandic saga

1

is regarded as necessarily a written work since it is "an artistic creation which far surpasses everything which one is accustomed to associate with the more primitive art of oral narrative."[5] No doubt this puts Homer, whose works are now generally accepted as being orally composed, in his place. For many literary men, illiteracy is still equated with lack of intelligence, ignorance of "culture." For these people, a narrative long since regarded as a "classic" (La Chanson de Roland, for example) can by no stretch of imagination be accepted as the product of illiterate minds. Forty years ago Milman Parry had this to say about the relation between oral and written poetry:

> ... it happened that the same man rarely knew
> both kinds of poetry, and if he did he was
> rather looking for that in which they were
> alike. That is, the men who were likely to
> meet with the songs of an unlettered people
> were not ordinarily of the sort who could
> judge soundly how good or bad they were, while
> the men with a literary background who
> published oral poems wanted above all to show
> that they were as good as [written] literature.[6]

This is certainly still true, but with the realization that traditional texts from many societies are, in fact, of oral origin the problem has become increasingly complex.

What are the fundamental differences between oral and literate cultures, and how are these differences reflected in the literature which each society produces? I think we may assume that literature reflects, in however indirect a form, the concerns and the mores of the society from which it comes. But more basic than explicit codes of behavior are the different ways in which a society regards its

environment, since these are outside the conscious control
of the literary composer. When considering the problem of
environment, however, we should always keep in mind that the
distinction between a literate and a non-literate society
may be extremely hard to draw -- there must be gradations in
between, and even in the medieval period societies which were
themselves illiterate had contact in one way or another with
those which were literate. Anthropologists following
Malinowski and Radcliffe-Brown, who worked on small islands,
have tried to duplicate their mentors' conditions in searching
for isolated communities, but have been forced to realize
that an apparently self-sufficient village is almost always
part of a much wider community. Likewise, in a modern
industrial society one finds subcultures of oral tradition,
which have become the domain of the modern folklorist and of
the student of popular culture.

The development of literacy brings about great changes
in the social structure of a group, but even before these
changes take place there are shifts in the perception of time
and space. Differences in social structure are manifested in
the literature of a society; changes in attitude to time and
space influence the literature at a deeper level. Thus, the
investigation of attitudes to time in medieval texts, supported
by an analysis of related stylistic differences, may well
prove useful in the comparison of oral and written literature.

For contrast let me begin with examples of the importance
of time in contemporary industrial society: the clock has been

called the key invention of the modern world.[7] Measurement
of time is essential to modern science and technology. The
manufacture of clocks (from the middle of the fifteenth
century) trained craftsmen in accurate mechanical models of
the universe, and enabled time to be alloted and organized
for particular tasks necessary to an industrial system. The
watch is often the first major gift a child, especially a
boy, receives, and it is often given at a significant point
in a person's life, such as the bar mitsvah, high school
graduation, twenty-first birthday, or retirement, marking
the accumulation of certain quantities of time. From at
least the middle of the nineteenth century when the cheap
watch began to be produced, to be as "regular as clockwork"
became the bourgeois ideal. Proverbial sayings regarding
time reveal the importance we attach to it: "time is money,"
"time and tide wait for no man," and so on. Time is seen as
passing irrevocably. It has become the focus of a status
symbol, as can be seen from any glossy magazine in which
advertisements link the expensive watch to success in the
social and especially the business worlk. Some watches sell
for prices comparable to that other symbol of modern society,
the automobile; "La Grande Complication" by Audemars Piguet
costs $25,000.

In a non-industrial society, however, the attitude
toward time is quite different:

> Time can be regarded as a recurring cycle.
> Certain events repeat themselves in definite
> sequence. This sequence is a continuity without
> beginning or end, and thus without any clear

distinction between past and present. The
most important time sequences are seasonal
activities and the passage of human life.
Both of these are conceived as of the same
kind. For such thinking, there is no
chronology, and time is not measureable.[8]

A study of word frequencies in different stages of
development of the French language demonstrates how different
social emphases are related to language: the twenty most
frequent nouns in La Chanson de Roland concern social rank
and battle, while in modern spoken French six of the first
seven most common nouns concern time, and ten out of the
first twenty.[9]

It is my purpose to discuss time in its psychological
and social aspects, to relate differences in the attitude
toward time in non-literate and literate societies to the
development of literacy and then to try to connect the
different concepts of time to the differences between the
kinds of literature produced by oral and literate societies.[10]

Time, like other categories of understanding, exists
only in the mind and is, in fact, a social construct related
to other aspects of social life: "all our thoughts and
concepts are called up by sense experience and have a meaning
only in reference to these sense experiences," as Albert
Einstein said.[11] Among African tribes such as the Nuer and
the Tiv "the notion that we call 'time' is not a separate
idea but an integral part of social activities and of
ecological and meteorological phenomena. Time is implicit in
Tiv thought and speech, but it is not a category of it."[12]

Our perception of time depends on our experience of

change, which includes sequence (the order of change) and the
duration of each change. Many of these changes, such as those
of light and darkness or the seasons, are part of our natural
environment, and both animals and man learn to synchronize
their lives in accordance with these natural rhythms. Our
bodies become conditioned to a particular recurring cycle of
day and night, abrupt change in which leads to fatigue and
discomfort such as that following intercontinental plane
travel. The subjective experience of duration is not
consistent but depends on activity; time seems to pass slowly
when we are idle but quickly when we are busy.[13]

According to Piaget,[14] it is not until adolescence that
we can separate the duration of unit changes from the concrete
nature of these changes, not until then can we conceptualize
time. From the age of eighteen months a child enlarges its
temporal horizon, and by the age of seven or eight reaches
beyond personal experience to develop a general idea of
history. Piaget, however, is discussing children of a
literate society, who from birth internalize the attitudes of
time of literate peers and elders. These ideas will be quite
different from those of a preliterate group. Again, we
cannot generalize for all from a study of a particular group.

The ideas of past and future are made precise by
language. Culture, of course, is transmitted by language,
and the structure of the language itself is significant.
Whorf,[15] who is criticized by contemporary anthropologists
as a linguistic determinist, said that the Hopi are incapable

of historicity because of the structure of their language.
Surely, however, language is rather a product of culture
than the other way round -- although obviously there is
reciprocity. For this reason verbal development seems to
take place in semantic fields of importance to a group:
Malinowski reported that in the Trobriands the outside world
was named only insofar as it yielded useful things.[16] The
language of the Eskimos and the tribes of New Guinea have
many words for fields of special interest, in the former
case for snow conditions and in the other for the varieties
of sweet potatoes. Medieval European epic contains many
words concerning warriors and battle. The Hopi have no
linguistic structures to represent history, as we understand
the term, since this is irrelevant to them; in their society,
as in many preliterate groups, there is an "eternal present."
This is a point to which we shall return.

One's temporal horizon is obviously linked to one's
way of life -- a peasant has no need to observe the precise
timing of a city-dweller -- and in a complex society this may
vary according to rank or role. Punctuality is not usually
as important for children and women as it is for men, and
technicians and businessmen are more likely to be on time
than literary critics. Yet even the most simple human group
is concerned with time to some extent. Seasonal activities,
the successful gathering of wild fruit and plants, and the
hunting of animals, depend on knowing where these are to be
found, and thus organization of time is necessary, particularly

the synchronization of the cycles of life with the cycles of
the cosmos.

Methods of reckoning sequence and duration vary according
to different factors and needs. The recording and measurement
of long periods of time are impossible without writing, the
acquisition of which closely linked to the linear concept of
time passing irrevocably which is emphasized in Judeo-
Christian thought and is fundamental to modern science and
history. Even though we live in an industrial society, we
still use both the cyclic and the linear concepts. The cyclic
idea of time is frequently connected to religious observances,
regularly recurring days of what Mircea Eliade calls "sacred
or festal time."[18] Our personal experience of time, subjective
time, is often in conflict with the rigid time set by our
industrial society; we may be enjoying ourselves or be busy
and time passes so quickly that we miss an appointment set
by clock-time. The years seem to pass slowly when we are
young but more quickly when we are older.

The concept and organization of time are basic to the
modern world, and the question arises whether variations in
these ideas are causally related to differences in individual
and technological development. According to the work of
Jack Goody, "it would appear that major changes in the concept
and organization of time follow rather than precede technological innovations" (Goody, 32).

All societies divide the day according to the periods
of light and darkness, and daylight is further divided in

relation to the changing position of the sun in the sky from dawn to dusk. Such changes are frequently linked to daily activities, and a time of day in which there is much activity will have more subdivisions than one when not much of importance in happening. For the Berens River Saulteaux, five terms describe that part of the day before the sun emerges into full view and another five almost the whole of the rest of the day: it is in the early day that the men lift their nets and check their traps.[19] Obviously, time-values which depend on the visibility of the sun and on activities such as hunting and fishing will vary with the season, the climate, and the presence or absence of game. For the Saulteaux the passage of time is indicated by a sequence of natural events which recur.

In medieval France also, the passage of time was connected to natural events -- or to the sound of a bell, itself linked to a natural cycle. Although Marc Bloch[20] refers to "a vast indifference to time" and says that the people of that age did not normally think in terms of the numbers of the years, one still meets with texts in which the canonical hours are translated into modern clock-time: prime allegedly is 6 a.m., tierce 9 a.m., sexte is noon, and none 3 p.m., or prime may also be given as the period of time between 6 a.m. and 9 a.m. The canonical hours of the Benedictine rule were, in fact, based on Roman computation which divided the day into twelve hours of daylight and twelve hours of darkness. Clearly, then, the length of an hour

depended on the time of year, and would only be sixty minutes
at the two equinoxes. The purpose of the canonical hours was
to indicate to the monks the day's activities, not to measure
time in any abstract way. There were fluctuations in these
times not only in any one monastery but also between one
order and another.[21] Nonetheless, a mechanical device was
being used to indicate the passage of time, and with the
division of the hour into minutes and seconds in the fourteenth century and the invention of the striking clock towards
the end of that century, the measurement of time was removed
completely from its connection with the natural world.[22]

The week is a social construct usually depending on
local markets and may vary from three to ten days. In Judaeo-
Christian societies it marks a shift from profane to sacred
because of the weekly break from ordinary matters during which
one should direct one's attention to other-worldly affairs.
The regular day of rest is of importance to the modern
industrial society also, and in England there is still some
prejudice against public recreation on Sunday.

Most societies use a month based originally on the lunar
cycle. Nonliterate groups pay particular attention to the
three-day period of the waning and waxing of the moon, which
is often connected with the cycle of human life and with
immortality, death and resurrection.

Some kind of yearly cycle, as well as the lunar one, is
important for groups involved in agriculture and hunting, but
without writing these cycles cannot be measured accurately.

The divisions of the year may be named according to the seasonal activities which themselves are obviously dependent on climactic conditions. Even in our technological society the farmer does not plant and harvest according to the calendar but rather when the time is ripe. In Iceland the year was divided into two main seasons, winter and summer, and although these were later connected to the ecclesiastical calendar, in earlier times they were clearly linked to seasonal activities. The names of the months reveal how closely the concept of time was connected to agriculture: "the first month of the summer half-year began in mid-April. It had two names, Cuckoo-month and Sowing-time ... mid-May to mid-June was called Egg (gathering)-time or Lambs'-fold-time."[23]

With the acquistion of writing, an accurate calendar becomes possible. However, the system based on the lunar cycle has to be reconciled to the solar cycle; intercalation becomes necessary as does the abandonment of purely lunar reckoning. In Iceland, intercalation was allegedly introduced by Thorstein the Wise in the second half of the tenth century. An extra week was added to the summer season every seventh year. In earlier times Icelanders had reckoned three hundred and sixty-four days in the year, fifty-two weeks.[24]

Writing also makes possible the reckoning of time from a fixed point in the past, and the concept of time becomes more linear, no longer repetitive. Such fixed points may be the birth of a prophet, the creation of the world, or the coming to power of a new political movement. Astronomy and mathematics can now develop, and the measurement of time becomes further removed from events such as the human and animal cycles and the growth of crops. Much social activity still depends on recurring festivals, however, and in agricultural societies these are linked to the beginning and end of the productive season, the solstice and the equinox. Although such festivals may be religious in origin, they are also meetings for the settling of disputes and debts of the arranging of marriages: "such events are often marked by a limited expression of tension between groups, although the likelihood of overt conflict is inhibited by ritual peace, supported by special sanctions against the outbreak of violence" (Goody, 36). This description of the functions of festivals fits very well the _Althing_ of Iceland, the annual meeting at midsummer which figures so importantly in many of the sagas.

The dissociation between human activities and the passage of time which is made possible by written calendars makes easier the spread of world religions in which the yearly cycle is connected to the life of the founder. It does not matter that Christmas is midwinter in the Northern Hemisphere but midsummer in the Southern since the anniversary of the birth of the prophet is no longer connected with the seasonal cycle. Such a religious basis for the calendar is also suitable for urban communities, which to a large extent are isolated from seasonal changes.

Like the year, the human life-cycle is divided into
smaller categories, such as infancy, adolescence, and
adulthood. The transition from one to another is often
marked by a rite of passage. Baptism follows birth; marriage
often follows some acceptance of the individual as an adult
with new rights and duties. The funeral is often the most
important ceremony in a non-industrial society since a man's
duties and rights, of property and office, have to be
transferred to other members of the community. Some of the
funerals in the sagas come to mind here.

Following the invention of writing and then the clock,
the precise allocation of time becomes possible: the clock
dominates the organization of our modern life, the world of
business, of government, of the military. For many people
the whole pattern of life is imposed from the outside by the
time-tables of trains or of the office, and even their
personal lives are ruled by schedules:

> The new bourgeoisie, in counting-house and shop,
> reduced life to a careful, uninterrupted routine:
> so long for business: so long for pleasure -- all
> carefully measured out, as methodical as the
> sexual intercourse of Tristram Shandy's father,
> which coincided, symbolically, with the monthly
> winding of the clock.[25]

As a society becomes more complex and a greater division
of labor occurs, a greater number of possible roles becomes
available to an individual. The selection among these involves
the allotment of time possibly over a whole lifetime, and
adults may feel that a wrong choice in their early years has
led to wasted time or even a wasted lifetime. In a less

differentiated society this kind of feeling is rare, since a
different choice would lead to a life much like the first.
For us who live in a complex society, the choice of career
depends on estimations concerning future conditions and
possible changes which would not occur to someone from a less
differentiated culture.

The importance of writing to modern civilization, as
has already been implied, can hardly be overestimated. Writing
is, of course, a method of communication which overcomes the
limits of oral tradition. The whole realm of human knowledge
is, theoretically at least, available to anyone who can read,
by means of the libraries of the great institutions of the
world. In an oral culture in which all knowledge is transmitted by the spoken word, knowledge is limited by memory.
All mathematics, science, technology, administration, and
money-making would be impossible without writing. The use
of writing completely changes the structure of a cultural
tradition.

The oral transmission of culture takes place essentially
through a series of face-to-face conversations, and in the
same way as a "singer of tales" adapts his story to the
reactions of his audience and other circumstances,[26] so the
whole of a society's outlook, its myths and legends, its
goals and aspirations, can be -- and are -- gradually and
unconsciously adapted to changing conditions. The anthropologist Laura Bohannan gives this example of what has been
called "structural amnesia":

> Early British administrators among the Tiv of
> Nigeria were aware of the great importance
> attached to genealogies and took the trouble
> to write down the long lists of names ... so
> that future administrators might refer to them
> in giving judgment. Forty years later ...
> their successors were still using the same
> geanealogies which now gave rise to many
> disagreements. The Tiv maintained that they
> were incorrect, while officials regarded them
> as statements of facts ... and could not agree
> that the unlettered indigenes could be better
> informed about the past than their own
> literate predecessors. What neither party
> realized was that in a society of this kind
> changes take place which require a constant
> readjustment in the genealogies if they are
> to carry out their function as mnemonics of
> social relationships (Goody and Watt, 32).

Another example given by Jack Goody concerns a state in
northern Ghana which is divided into seven chiefdoms. Early
in the twentieth century it was said that the founder of the
state, Jakpa, had come down from the north, conquered the
local people, and begotten seven sons who became the rulers
of seven chiefdoms. Sixty years later when the myths were
again reported, two of these seven divisions had disappeared,
one because it had been absorbed by a neighboring group and
another because of administrative changes introduced by the
British. At this time, Jakpa was said to have had five sons,
no mention being made of the founders of the two groups which
had since split off. Jonathan Miller analyzes this function
of oral tradition thus:

> Memory ... is an editorial ministry which
> reconstructs its past experience in accordance
> with the peculiar needs of the imagination.
> Therefore the past which an oral culture shapes
> for itself tells us more about the collective
> mentality of the group than it does about the
> historical reality to which its constituent
> memories supposedly refer.[27]

Oral tradition, therefore, is flexible enough to adapt to changing conditions and reflects the structure and attitudes of the contemporary society rather than being an accurate record. As Erich Auerbach remarks, "for audiences of the eleventh, twelfth, and thirteenth centuries the heroic epic was history ... no other tradition existed, at least none accessible to those audiences. It is only about the year 1200 that the first vernacular chronicles are composed."[28] Until this time whatever chronicles were written were in Latin. From the anthropological examples given, then, one would expect the epic to reflect the conditions of the time of its recording in writing and not those of the period it is allegedly reporting.

In a society with written records, of course, this flexibility is not possible. Changes in social attitude can only be mirrored in the law, for example, by having the legislative body "re-write" the law. In a country such as the United States with a written constitution, a constitutional amendment may have to be passed by the legislature, or a progressive interpretation by a single judge may have to be upheld by the federal Supreme Court. Since written records can be consulted by any literate person, the differences between "the law" and ordinary behavior can be easily seen and can lead to skepticism with regard to social institutions and the development of a more individualized consciousness. Thought may become empirical and more objective. The world religions that are religions of "the book" are open to similar criticism. Reinterpretations of the texts from literal to parable to allegory may become necessary. The individual path to salvation is stressed in these religions, but skepticism is also possible among literate believers if the text is available, for a comparison of the doctrine with the Church's teaching and its representative may reveal some discrepancy.

In medieval Europe, of course, the mass of the population was illiterate and teaching was mostly oral. Marc Bloch suggests that although some of the great princes and members of the great families were literate, "north of the Alps and the Pyrenees at least the majority of the small and medium lords who exercised most authority ... were illiterate in the full sense of the word. ...it is important to realize that the decisions of the powerful of this world were sometimes suggested and always expressed ... by the clergy."[29] In many cases, of course, the clergy would have to translate as well as read any documents. Chaucer's Canterbury Tales give many examples both of the corruption of Christian ideals and of the oral methods of teaching.

In a partly literate society there can develop great differences between the literate -- the ruling class and its advisers -- and the illiterate. As culture begins to be transmitted in writing, those who cannot read may be excluded from parts of it, while in a purely oral culture every member of the group has equal access to the tradition. The tendency of the oral tradition is to be an expression of ideas and

attitudes of the group rather than the individual. C. M.
Bowra refers to La Chanson de Roland in these terms, regarding
it as "an archetype of all battles against the heathen" and
showing "the spirit in which the crusaders of the twelfth
century set about their task of war."[30] Not only does Bowra
see the epic in terms of the group but he also believes that
oral poetry reflects contemporary social conditions rather
than those of the earlier society supposedly described.

One of the most important consequences of literacy
concerns history, the sense of the past. As we have seen,
an oral culture adapts to its circumstances with little
consciousness of time passing. Without written records
accurate evidence of the past is scanty, since even oral
records to which great importance may be attached, such as
genealogies, rarely extend over more than a few generations.
Once written records begin to be kept, a sense of the past,
a sense of "history," may arise and references to past events
can be more exact. The early Greek historian Herodotus based
his work on traditional oral tales which contained many mythic
elements, but Thucydides made a decisive effort to separate
myth from history:

> This meant that unverified assumptions about the
> past had to be excluded. So Thucydides ...
> confined himself very largely to his own notes
> of the events and speeches he related, or to the
> information he sought out from eyewitnesses and
> other reliable sources. (Goody and Watt, 47-48)

As a result of this kind of historical writing, a very
different attitude toward the past, toward the traditional
cultural repetoire emerged. Inconsistencies became obvious

and thus people were forced to take a much more careful look
at their society's concepts and ideals. The past of a society
which has written records extends linearly from the present
moment back to the time when the first event was recorded.
Time can be envisaged as a sequence beginning at a fixed
point in the past and continuing through the present into the
future. For an oral culture in which the social attributes
are unconsciously but always changing, the secular past can
only be seen in terms of present circumstances. The mythic
past, on the other hand, is used as a kind of mirror in which
present and future are reflected. Time, therefore, is seen
in terms of recurring or repetitive situations, closely linked
to the consmic or human cycles which are experienced by the
group and with which their regular activities are synchronized.

Just as there are still some literary men who cannot
accept the idea that illiterate poets can produce narratives
of great power and beauty, so there are still people who
cannot believe that members of a "primitive" society are
capable of "logical" thinking. Goody and Watt mention Cassirer
as assuming "an absolute and untenable dichotomy between the
'mythical' thought of primitives and the 'logico-empirical'
though of civilized man" (Goody and Watt, 43). We have
generally got beyond the point of regarding pre-literate
societies as using "pre-logical" thinking -- both Lévi-Strauss
and Evans-Pritchard have done work on the logic of pre-
literate groups[31] -- but, nevertheless, it seems clear that
writing establishes a more general and abstract relationship

between the word and its referent, that the written word is less closely connected to concrete reality. With written literature, for example, there is the possibility of the accumulation of layers of meanings and associations unlikely with oral literature. As McLuhan says, "to the oral man the literal is inclusive, contains all possible meanings and levels,"[32] and Spengler remarks that "writing implies a complete change in man's waking consciousness, in that it liberates him from the tyranny of the present; ... the activity of writing and reading is infinitely more abstract than of speaking and hearing."[33] Thus, the more one contemplates these differences, the more one becomes aware that the application of modern techniques of literary criticism developed for and by a written tradition to largely oral works such as La Chanson de Roland is essentially inappropriate. A different system of literary appreciation must be developed for oral literature, stressing tradition perhaps rather than originality.

Writing, suggest Goody and Watt, makes abstract thought possible to a greater degree than does oral tradition and leads to the organization of knowledge into separate intellectual disciplines, to the fractionation of experience. In fifth century Athens most of the citizens could read the laws, and by the time of the death of Aristotle in 322 BC "most of the categories in the fields of philosophy, natural sciences, language and literature had been delineated and the systematic collection and classification of data in all of them had

begun" (Goody and Watt, 54-55). Among the fields of inquiry
beginning at this period was theology, dividing the human,
natural world from the supernatural, a separation unknown
among illiterate people.

With the accumulation of the past in written records,
the totality of the culture increases. It becomes impossible
for a single individual, even if he is literate, to take part
in every aspect of social and cultural life, and if he is not
literate, he is inevitably excluded from at least some
activities. From the unified structure of a pre-literate
group, an increasingly literate society becomes increasingly
stratified. An ever growing number of choices become available to the individual which may augment social mobility, or,
if the social structure is rigid, increase alienation. Each
individual is likely at different ages to embody different
layers of beliefs and attitudes corresponding to the general
beliefs of his peers. The past may mean different things to
different groups within a society: for the ruling class there
may be nostalgia for "the good old days" which for the ruled
meant nothing but want and hardship.

Even in a literate society the oral tradition is an
important part of the transmission of culture. Although a
child may learn historical approach from its parents, a
great deal of learning takes place in the peer group and this,
of course, is oral. A study of children's songs and games,
such as that of the Opies, shows how strong oral traditions
still are.[34] There may well arise a serious conflict between

what is learned from the oral tradition and what is learned
from the official sources of the society -- that is, what is
taught in school. This contrast was clearly pointed out by
Margaret Mead: "Primitive education was a process by which
continuity was maintained ... modern education includes a
heavy emphasis upon the function of education to create dis-
continuities -- to turn the child of the illiterate into the
literate."[35] For "primitive education" read "oral education,"
and for "modern education" read "literate tradition," and we
have the kind of contrasts I have been discussing.

The discontinuity of a literate group is seen in the
image of a person reading a book, silent and solitary. One
can learn by oneself; one has no need of the rest of the
group. But in an oral culture one can learn nothing by oneself; the group is vital. On the one hand is independence
and potential criticism, and on the other dependence and
acceptance. Writing encourages private thought which, since
it is more abstract, is less connected with personal experience.
Ideas which are given permanency in writing are available for
consideration over a considerable period of time. Clearly,
an oral culture in which almost every situation brings the
individual into contact with a traditional pattern of behavior may be described, as by Durkheim, as having "mechanical
solidarity,"[36] while in a literate group individualization is
more likely and each person has, potentially at least, more
freedom of action and of thought.

Printing so obviously makes knowledge accessible

> to all that we are inclined to forget that it
> also makes knowledge very easy to avoid ... A
> shepherd in an Icelandic homestead, on the
> other hand, could not avoid spending his
> evenings listening to the kind of literature
> which interested the farmer. The result was
> a degree of really national culture such as
> no nation of today has been able to achieve.[37]

The unity of culture to which Bertha Phillpotts refers here

is, of course, precisely the kind of unity typical of an

oral culture.

Clearly, then, literacy has many consequences for a

society's way of thinking and can strongly affect concepts of

time. It remains to explore differences in the style of the

literary products of these two types of society and the

relations of these differences to different time concepts.

The work of H. and A. Thornton, Time and Style,[38] a work

which never mentions literacy, demonstrates style changes

occurring in Greek literature of the fourth century BC in

relation to the concept of time. This same change is dis-

cussed by Goody and Watt in the study I have discussed earlier,

and is quite definitely connected by them with the rise of

literacy. The Thorntons' findings, however, especially since

they cover literature from Homer to Virgil, can be coordinated

well with the ideas I have already mentioned, and this syn-

cretic theory can then be applied to the medieval works I

plan to consider.

Let me begin by summarizing the Thorntons' findings.

The style of early Greek and Latin authors they have chosen

is characterized as largely "appositional." The generally

paratactic style contains both "linear" and "appositional"

elements, the appositional consisting of "a plain, but emphatic initial statement of the main item of the sentence or passage; expansions of this initial statement which elaborate it in a variety of syntactical forms; and, frequently, a return to the initial statement" (Thornton, xi). This style has been described as "Homer's normal method of exposition,"[39] and an excellent example of it -- though one which the Thorntons do not use -- is given by Auerbach in his chapter "Odysseus' scar."[40] Auerbach discusses the story of the origin of the scar, an episode of seventy verses, which interrupts the recognition of Odysseus by Euryclea. All such similar "retardations" take place, says Auerbach, in the foreground, "in a local and temporal present which is absolute. One might think that the many interpolations ... would create a sort of perspective in time and place, but the Homeric style ... knows only foreground, only a uniformly illuminated, uniformly objective present." This idea of a uniformly objective present seems very close to the sense of time of an oral culture, a culture itself unconscious of change, which views the secular past in terms of the present, and its own culture as unchanging. "In the appositional style the past is felt and experienced so vividly that it seems little removed from the present. Time as implied in it is not clearly or necessarily differentiated into past, present, and future" (Thornton, 86). The audience perceives the continuity of its tradition; the epic extols the greatness of previous generations and holds them up as models for the present with little sense of the "pastness" of the past.

The appositional style is found to predominate in Greek authors at least up to Pindar, but in Pindar a different kind of expression is sometimes found, "one in which, owing to the word order, the tension of looking forward expectantly towards what is to come characterizes the movement of thought (Thornton, 71). In Herodotus both modes appear, although the appositional is used in the composition of the longer passages, while in Thucydides the style producing expectation is more common. Goody and Watt suggest that Herodotus used many oral sources which gave his work a mythic content while Thucydides relied on his own observations as much as possible and thus his work was more "historical."

I have already discussed the importance of literacy in making possible the idea of the past as different from the present, the linear concept of time, and the writing of history. By taking together the evidence of Goody and Watt and that of the Thorntons, we can make a connection between the change from appositional style and the development of literacy: The appositional style may well be a characteristic of oral literature. One would also expect there to be a connection between this change in literary style and changes in the concept and treatment of time. This certainly seems to be the case according to the Thorntons' study.

To summarize, time in pre-literate societies is not abstract, conceptual, but its passage is connected to events -- the cosmic cycle, recurrent seasonal activities, and so on.

It is not seen as continuous and there is little sense of
the historic past or the future. Duration and change are
experienced by each individual, however, but are qualitative
-- the passage of time is experienced only according to the
person's feelings and activities.

From anthropological and literary evidence it appears
therefore that the advent of writing produces great changes
in a society and its culture, one of the most fundamental
being a change in the concept of time. It seems very likely
that such a change will be reflected not only in the way time
is considered in literature but in the very literary style
itself.

The texts I shall use to test these possibilities are:
in Old French La Chanson de Roland and Chrétien's Yvain; in
Old Norse Atlakviða and Gunnlaugs Saga; in English Beowulf,
Sir Gawain and the Green Knight, and Chaucer's "The Shipman's
Tale." The first two pairs contrast respectively epic and
romance, heroic lays and romantic saga, and the last group an
early heroic poem, a romance, and a fabliau.

La Chanson de Roland is one of the oldest of the
chansons de gestes and is of oral composition, while Yvain
is the highly literary product of a known author. Atlakviða
is very early, recognized as oral in origin, and contrasts
with the late thirteenth century saga of Gunnlaug. Beowulf
is the only long heroic poem in English, while Sir Gawain and
the Green Knight has some interesting transitional qualities.
In the Canterbury tale I wish to see whether the social

setting of the poem affects the treatment of time. Chaucer no doubt understood that in the bourgeois setting of the Shipman's tale time was money.

It is important to remember that even the literary products of the medieval period were in manuscript, not print, and were more frequently recited to an audience than read individually and silently. In fact, the generally accepted view seems to be that the medieval reader did not read as we do. As H. J. Chaytor says,

> he was in the stage of our muttering childhood learner; each word was for him a separate entity which he whispered to himself when he had found the solution ... When we take up a printed edition of a medieval text ... we bring unconsciously to its perusal those prejudices and prepossessions which years of association with printed matter have made habitual.[41]

The medieval world was closer to oral tradition, even when literate, than it was to our world of print. To adapt another remark of Chaytor's we can say that if we wish to pass a fair judgment on oral literature, we must make an effort to suspend the prejudices of our literate and technological backgrounds.

NOTES

[1]However, despite the 20th century obsessions with "scientific" accuracy, even this work has frequently left much to be desired. See Joseph J. Duggan, The Song of Roland: Formulaic Style and Poetic Craft (Berkeley and Los Angeles: University of California Press, 1973), p. 16ff., for a review and criticism of many studies, for example, Diamond, Magoun, and Benson on Old English, Parry and Lord on Greek, and various studies on Old French.

[2]Albert B. Lord, The Singer of Tales (Cambridge: Harvard University Press, 1960).

[3]Duggan, The Song of Roland; James A. Notopoulos, "Parataxis in Homer: A New Approach to Homeric Literary Criticism," TAPA, 80 (1949), 1-23.

[4]W. P. Ker, Epic and Romance (London: Macmillan, 1908; New York: Dover, 1957); C. M. Bowra, Heroic Poetry (London: Macmillan, 1952); Eugene Vinaver, The Rise of Romance (Oxford: Clarendon, 1971).

[5]This comment by Sigurdur Nordal is quoted in Peter Hallberg's The Icelandic Saga (Lincoln: University of Nebraska Press, 1962), p. 67. The remark of Nordal's is in relation to his attack on the so-called "free prose theory" (i.e., oral tradition) of the origin of the Icelandic "Saga of Icelanders." The free prose theorists maintain that the sagas have preserved a historical tradition from the tenth century

when they were composed to the thirteenth century when they
were written down. In his attack, Nordal points out that
two of the characters in Hrafnkel's Saga did not exist
according to the Landnámabók. This is a serious blow for the
free prose theorists since Hrafnkel's Saga is usually taken
as one of the more historical sagas. But Landnámabók (the
Book of Settlements, which allegedly describes the first
settlers in Iceland from the end of the ninth century) itself
was compiled "as early (sic) as the twelfth century" according
to Hallberg (p. 5). Presumably, then, either Landnámabók is
based on oral tradition or it must be pure fiction: in neither
case can it be used as a standard by which to judge the
accuracy of a saga. Nordal betrays himself with the comment
on the "primitive art of oral narrative."

[6]Albert B. Lord, "Homer, Parry, and Huso," American
Journal of Archeology, 52 (1942), 37.

[7]Lewis Mumford, Technics and Civilization (New York:
Harcourt Brace, 1934).

[8]E. R. Leach, "Primitive Time-Reckoning," in A History
of Technology, C. J. Singer, E. J. Holmyard, and A. R. Hall,
eds., (Oxford: Clarendon, 1958), p. 114.

[9]G. Gougenheim, "Récherches sur la Frequence et la
disponsibilité," Colloque de Strasbourg 1964, Statistique et
Analyse Linguistic, (Presses Universitaires de France, 1966),
pp. 57-66.

[10]The succeeding sections depend heavily on the following
articles and books: Paul Fraisse, "Time: psychological aspects,"

in The International Encyclopedia of the Social Sciences,
E. R. A. Seligman and A. Johnson, eds., (New York: Macmillan,
1968), Vol. 16, 25-30; Jack Goody, "Time: social organization,"
in The International Encyclopedia of the Social Sciences, Vol.
7, 30-41; Jack Goody and Ian Watt, "The Consequences of
Literacy," in Literacy in Traditional Societies (Cambridge:
The University Press, 1968); H. and A. Thornton, Time and
Style (London: Methuen, 1962). Direct quotations will be
followed by the author's name and the page number, e.g.,
(Goody and Watt, 34).

[11]Albert Einstein, "Space-Time," in Encyclopedia Brittanica (Chicago: Encyclopedia Brittanica, 1973), Vol. 20, 1070.

[12]Paul Bohannan, "Concepts of Time among the Tiv of
Nigeria," Southwestern Journal of Anthropology, 9 (1953),
251-62.

[13]Michel Siffre, a French speleologist, estimated his
stay in an underground cavern to have been only thirty-three
days although he had had fifty-eight periods of sleep. His
sleep records were a much more accurate indication than his
calculations. See also Jack Vernon, Inside the Black Room
(London: Penguin, 1966), chapter six, "Sense deprivation and
orientation in Time."

[14]Jean Piaget, The Child's Concept of Time (New York:
Ballantine, 1968).

[15]B. J. Whorf, Language, Thought and Reality (Cambridge:
M.I.T. Press, 1956), pp. 153ff. Also in Goody and Watt, pp.
64-65.

[16]Quoted in Goody and Watt, p. 29. Dorothy D. Lee, "Codifications of Reality: Lineal and Non-lineal," in *Freedom and Culture* (Englewood Cliffs, New Jersey: Prentice Hall, 1959), pp. 105-120.

[17]Georges Gurvitch, "Structures sociales et multiplicité des temps," *Bulletin de la Société de Philosophie Française*, 52 (1958); Margaret Mead, ed., *Cultural Patterns and Technical Change* (Paris: UNESCO, 1953).

[18]Mircea Eliade, *The Sacred and the Profane*, tr. W. R. Trask (New York: Harcourt Brace, 1959), p. 71.

[19]A. Irving Hallowell, "Temporal Orientation in Western Civilization and in a Pre-literate Society," *American Anthropologist*, 39 (1937), no. 4.

[20]Marc Bloch, *Feudal Society*, tr. L. A. Manyon (Chicago: University of Chicago Press, 1962), pp. 74, 84.

[21]W. Rothwell, "The Hours of the Day in Medieval French," *French Studies*, 13 (1959), 240-51.

[22]George Sarton, *Introduction to the History of Science* (Baltimore: Williams and Wilkins, 1953), Vol. III, 716-22.

[23]Jacqueline Simpson, *Everyday Life in the Viking Age* (London: Carousel, 1971), pp. 67ff.

[24]Magnus Magnusson and Herman Pálsson, eds. and trs., *Laxdaela Saga* (London: Penguin, 1959), p. 55.

[25]Mumford, *Technics and Civilization*, p. 42.

[26]Albert B. Lord, *The Singer of Tales*, p. 23.

[27]Jonathan Miller, *McLuhan* (London: Fontana, 1971), p. 87.

[28]Erich Auerbach, _Mimesis_, tr. W. R. Trask (Princeton, N.J.: Princeton University Press, 1968), p. 122.

[29]Marc Bloch, _Feudal Society_, pp. 80ff.

[30]C. M. Bowra, _Heroic Poetry_, p. 520.

[31]Claude Lévi-Strauss, _The Savage Mind_ (Chicago: University of Chicago Press, 1966), pp. 48ff.: "the logic of totemic classifications." E. E. Evans-Prtichard, _Witchraft, Oracles, and Magic among the Azande_ (Ocford: Clarendon, 1937); "the logical nature of the belief-systems of the Azande of the Sudan."

[32]Marshall McLuhan, _The Gutenburg Galaxy_ (Toronto: University of Toronto Press, 1962; New York: New American Library, 1969), p. 137.

[33]Oswald Spengler, _The Decline of the West_, tr. C. F. Atkinson (New York: Knopf, 1934), Vol. II, 149.

[34]Iona and Peter Opie, _Lore and Language of Schoolchildren_ (Oxford: Clarendon, 1959).

[35]Margaret Mead, _Cultural Patterns_, p. 9.

[36]Emil Durkheim, _The Division of Labor in Society_, tr. G. S. Simpson (New York: Glencoe Free Press, 1933), p. 130.

[37]Bertha Phillpotts, _Edda and Saga_ (London: Butterworth, 1931), pp. 162-63.

[38]H. and A. Thornton, _Time and Style_.

[39]S. E. Bassett, _The Poetry of Homer_ (Berkeley and Los University of California Press, 1938), Sather Classical Lecture, Vol. 15, 150ff.

[40]Erich Auerbach, _Mimesis_, pp. 3ff.

[41]H. J. Chaytor, _From Script to Print_ (Cambridge: Heffer and Son, 1945), p. 10.

[42]For an excellent discussion of the differences between oral and written literature, as well as a plea for oral literary criticism, see Alan Dundes, Oral Literature," in James A. Clifton, ed., _Introduction to Cultural Anthropology_ (Boston: Houghton Miflin, 1968), pp. 117-29; Alan Dundes, ed., _The Study of Folklore_ (Englewood Cliffs, New Jersey: Prentice-Hall, 1964).

Chapter II

ACCOUNTING FOR TIME: EARLY TEXTS

In non-literate societies the significance of changes
in Nature, such as those of the seasons and celestial events,
is preserved by word of mouth as part of the oral cultural
heritage. Some assistance may be given by the use of marks
on sticks or carved figures, or the building of structures in
which the change in length of the shadow of a vertical pillar
is noted and marked at different times of the year -- such as
the solstices and equinoxes -- and moveable markers may be
used in the prediction of other celestial events. Many of
the prehistoric structures of Europe are now thought by many
scholars to be sophisticated instruments for astronomical
observations.[1]

With the development of writing elaborate records may
be kept and more accurate divisions of time-periods made, and
writing is used for other accounting purposes -- for inven-
tories of property, trade figures, taxes, and other kinds of
accounts.[2]

But in a non-literate society the precise measurement
of time has no significance in ordinary daily activities --
agriculture and the hunt are only carried out when the time
is ripe., not at the artificial bidding of a mechanical device.
For ritual, however, the observation of time may be important,
but this religious time is separate from secular existence.
Generally speaking, time is of little account particularly
in the narratives of such a society.

Technological societies, however, regard time in
literature quite differently:

> We look nowadays upon a narrative of events
> as a _temporal_ sequence, each element of which
> moves towards the next as each moment of time
> moves towards the one that follows; and at the
> same time we see it as a _rational_ sequence so
> arranged that each phrase of it is related in
> a definable manner to whatever comes before or
> after. What is so difficult for us to under-
> stand is that a great masterpiece such as
> the _Song of Roland_ should triumphantly dis-
> card the twin principles of rational and
> temporal motivation.[3]

W. P. Ker says that "_Roland_ is a succession of separate scenes
with no gradation between them" and quotes Gaston Paris who
refers to the _Roland_ as developing "par une suite d'explosions
successives."[4] Erich Auerbach remarks of _Roland_:

> Every line marks a new start, every stanza
> represents a new approach ... the entire
> strophe appears to be a bundle of independent
> parts as though sticks or spears of equal
> lengths and with similar points were bundled
> together ... [The _Roland_] strings independent
> pictures together like beads ... in such a
> fashion that ... completely independent and
> self-contained scenes result.[5]

The emphasis of these critics is on the discontinuity of the
narrative, and Auerbach adds that the paratactic constructions
of the _Roland_ "in the classical languages ... belong to the
low style: they are oral rather than written."[6] The _Song of
Roland_ has been shown convincingly, by J. J. Duggan,[7] to be
orally composed: perhaps the lack of the kind of continuity
we expect in modern narrative is one of the characteristics
of oral poetry.

In the _Roland_, although Charlemagne has to travel some
distance to the aid of Roland under attack, the question of

whether he will reach he nephew's side in time in not ex-
ploited by the poet. The knights express a wish to help
Roland before he dies but the poet tells us that it is already
too late. As the army returns to Spain, the knights say to
each other:

> "Se veïssum Rollant ainz qu'il fust mort
>
> Ensembl'od lui i durriums granz colps"

But the poet adds: "De ço qui calt? car demuret i unt trop"
(1804-06). Charlemagne prays that God will look after Roland
until they reach him, but again the poet adds: "De ço qui
calt? car ne lur valt nient Demuret trop, n'i poedent estre
a tens" (1840-41). The poet ignores the opportunity to
create a great deal of tension and expectation in his audience;
one can imagine how this scene would be treated in a movie.

Before we go any further in our discussion of the poem's
chronology, we should consider some general points concerning
"realism." As members of a technological society with a long
history of literary culture, we have become accustomed to
equate the effectiveness with which reality is conveyed to us
as a measure, if not _the_ measure, of literary excellence.
Fundamental to our ideas of reality are plausibility of number, time, and space -- perhaps not unconnected to the
dramatic unities of time, place, and action. But to appreciate
the value of a narrative which comes from a non-technological
setting we must learn to discard our literate prejudices, our
feelings of superiority to the illiterates who produced oral
epics such as the _Roland_.

We must accept that their cultural emphases were on other aspects of the narratives than ours would be.

The first example of "unreality" which probably strikes a reader is the large and changing number of troops which take part in the battles and journeys. When Charlemagne begins his return to Spain sixty thousand trumpets sound (2111), and at Roncevaux twenty thousand men faint on seeing the battlefield (2416). In the Baligant episode, the Emir has thirty divisions, the least of which contains fifty thousand men -- a total of more than one and a half million (3217-19). Charlemagne is said to be more than two hundred years old (524) and Baligant is older than Virgil and Homer. Are we to take these figures literally? One is perhaps at first amused and then one ignores the exaggerations and inconsistencies. Neither reaction is in keeping with twelfth century taste.

With space and time, however, the question of realism seems harder to deal with. We know that the poem is based on a historical event of August 15, 778, so perhaps that is the reason that critics have spent a great deal of ink and in-genuity in trying to reconcile the text of the poem with the geography of Spain.

We are told in the first laisse that the Saracen leader, Marsile, holds Saragossa (6), and later that Charlemagne has taken "Cordres." Cordova is the city which seems to be in-dicated, but Saragossa is in the north while Cordova is some four hundred miles away to the south. To travel from one to

to the other in the eighth century would take weeks but there
is no reference to this in the poem so some scholars have
tried to find another town closer to Saragossa for "Cordres."
P. Boissonnade[8] has suggested the small town of Cortes which
is not far from Saragossa, and thinks it is necessary to
accept this since "c'est seulement dans un conte des féés
que le trajet entre Cordoue et l'Erbe pouvait être accompli
en un laps de temps aussi court." This seems to be an in-
adequate reason for tampering with the text. Any competent
folklorist could have told Boissonnade that the names in a
traditional narrative are not intended to represent reality
with exactitude. Menéndez-Pídal is almost alone in suggesting
that most of the place-names used in the Roland are "fabu-
leux."[9] The fact that much energy has been expended in
attempts to reconcile the poem with the hard facts seems to
show how deeply ingrained in modern man is the sense of the
reality of time and space -- a sense which, I submit, was
not so ingrained in the mentality of a still largely pre-
literate culture.

Let us see, then, how time is accounted for in the
Roland. We are told at the beginning of the poem that
Charlemagne has been in Spain for seven years. The time
seems to be the epic present -- Charlemagne is "nostre emperere," and we are told that Saragossa is held by Marsile;
"li reis Marsile la tient." The council of Marsile takes
place, the convoy leaves and arrives at Charlemagne's court
at "Cordres" with no reference to the passage of time. After

greetings are exchanged there is an indication of the time
of day, although an imprecise one: "bels fut li vespres e li
soleilz fut cler" (157).

Night falls and in the early morning Charlemagne hears
Mass and Matins and holds his council. Decisions are taken
and Ganelon leaves to meet the pagans and rides with them to
Saragossa, presumably from Cordova. Another example of the
poet's lack of interest in suspense occurs here: at our
introduction to Ganelon we are at once told that he is the
villain of the piece -- "Guenes i vint, ki la traïsun fist"
(178); later it is clear that Charlemagne is aware of this
since he says, after a prophetic dream, "par Guenelun serait
destruite France" (835). But this knowledge has no effect
on the action.

The last lap of Ganelon's journey back to Charlemagne
ends at night (how many days and nights the whole journey
takes we are not told) since he catches up with the army at
dawn: "Par main en l'albe, si cum li jurz esclairet" (667).
The meeting is at "Galne," which has not been identified.
The French leave for "dulce France" and march till nightfall,
presumably to Roncevaux since the next morning Roland is
designated leader of the rearguard and the main army moves
on towards France. As they march, Charlemagne tells Naimes
of his ominous dream, his feeling that Ganelon has betrayed
him for bribes received from the pagans. In the middle of
this laisse (68) we suddenly read that Marsile has ordered
troops collected from all over Spain and in three days four

hundred thousand men have come together:

> Marsilies mandet d'Espaigne les baruns
>
> Cuntes, vezcuntes e dux e almaçurs,
>
> Les amirafles e les filz as cunturs:
>
> .III. C. milie en ajustet en .III. jurz
>
> (848-851)

When was this order of Marsile's given? Is one to assume
that Marsile went into action as soon as Ganelon left him?
Even if this is so, the Saracens have to move unrealistically
fast, since there is no indication that Roland has to wait
long before the battle begins. The leaders of Marsile's
forces announce themselves, the weather is fine ("clers fut
li jurz e bels fut li soleilz" [1002]), Roland refuses to
sound his horn, and the two armies meet.

Already it has become impossible to construct a time-
table of the action, partly because of the lack of precision
over the Saracens' movements, and also because there is no
way of telling how long the various journeys have taken.
There is no effort made to coordinate the events, no attempt
at verisimilitude in time. The expression "III jurz" is then
merely an indication of a relatively brief period of time.

While the battle continues a great storm arises in
France so that people think it is the end of the world ("la
fin del secle" [1435]), and "cuntre midi tenebres i ad granz"
(1431). One may assume here, I think, that the time indication
is not precise since the storm obviously has some duration:
"in the middle of the day" may be an acceptable English

equivalent, rather than "at noon."

When Roland finally blows his horn (1753), Charlemagne
and his army are still in the mountains ("as porz passant"
[1767]) although before the battle began they were in sight
of Gascony ("Virent Guascuigne, la tere lur seignur" [819]),
and as the sound of the horn reaches Charlemagne, Ganelon
says that "Tere Major mult est loin ça devant (1784). Again,
there is a lack of coordination.

The battle has lasted some time, for "esclargiz est li
vestres e li jurz" (1807), but how much is uncertain. The
main force hopes to reach Roland before his death so they can
join him in dealing death to the infidels, but, as we have
discussed above, they cannot do so. As Charlemagne hears
Roland's last weakened blast on his horn, he gives the orders
for his trumpeters to answer; the pagans hear with terror,
and flee "envers Espaigne" (2165). But Roland and the rearguard were left "en Espaigne" (826). This does, however,
seem to be a vague spatial reference.

Roland is dead when the emperor reaches Roncevaux, and
Naimes tells Charlemagne that the enemy is only two leagues
away, judging by the dust-clouds. At first this is thought
to be too far for pursuit, but after Charlemagne gives orders
for the burial of the dead, the French army sets off after
the Saracens. Night begins to fall -- "le vespres decliner"
(2447) -- so the emperor prays that the sun may stop: "li
soleilz ... arester,/ La nuit targer e le jur demurer"
(2449-50), and God grants the request. The battle, therefore,

seems to have lasted for most of one day -- if it is possible
for the French army to have gotten from wherever they were
to wherever Roland was.

The sun stops, the pagans are slaughtered or drowned,
and when all the enemy are killed -- which would take a
considerable time -- Charlemagne gives thanks to God on his
knees. When he rises, "li soleilz est culchet./ Dist l'emperere: 'Tens est del herberger'/ En Rencesvals est tart de
repairer" (2481-83). The Franks camp presumably near the
river Ebro; the army sleeps and Charlemagne dreams.

Marsile has fled to Saragossa having been wounded in
the battle, but the temporal relation between his flight and
the previous events is not given. As he and his men curse
their fate, we have a flashback. There is a repetition of
the first laisse: we are told again that Charlemagne was in
Spain for seven years, but now we hear that in the first of
these years Marsile had sent letters to the Emir of Babylon,
Baligant. In the letters, Marsile begged for help, and swore
that he would renounce his gods and make peace with Charlemagne if the Emir did not come to his assistance (2613-21).
Apparently, the Emir had taken six years to prepare, but as
these events were taking place, Baligant was setting out;
"Ço est en mai, al premer jur d'ested" (2628) that the fleet
is launched from Alexandria. We are thus given some idea
of the time of year for the first time when the poem is
almost two-thirds gone, although we could assume that it was
summer -- from indications such as the clouds of dust raised

by the fleeing pagans -- and that summer was the usual campaign
season. But if Baligant leaves Alexandria sometime in May,
when would he arrive in Saragossa? One would have to allow
several weeks since the direct distance is almost one thousand
eight hundred miles, and in the eighth century the ships
would no doubt cling to the shore. So, from this evidence,
late summer is as close as we can get to the placing of the
events of the poem in time; the duration of the events is
not, however, affected, and this is what we are concerned
with at the moment.

The news of the Emir's approaching fleet reaches Marsile,
and the ships arrive at Saragossa at dawn. The day, naturally,
is "clers" and the sun "luisant" (2646), and it is precisely
the day after Charlemagne's great victory since Marsile tells
Baligant's envoys that he son was slain "her seir" (2745).
This is almost the only occasion in which there is a time-
relation between one day and the next, and it is followed in
the same laisse by a remark of Marsile's which also gives an
explicit time-reference: he says that, with Baligant's help,
they will have conquered the French within a month. "Cunquis
l'avrat d'oi cest jur en un meis" (2751). The following
laisse tells us that Charlemagne is camped "anuit" on the
banks of the Ebro, only seven leagues away. The messengers
return to Baligant and tell the story of the Saracen defeat,
mentioning that it occurred "ier" (2771) and repeating this
information twenty verses later. The proximity of the French
is mentioned and the attack upon them is planned.

Charlemagne awakes "al matin, quant primes pert li albe" (2845) and with the army returns to Roncevaux, which would in reality take several days -- but this is not referred to. The corpses still lie where they fell. Some thousands are laid to rest and as soon as this is done the messengers of the Emir arrive with a challenge to battle; there is still enough time to complete a military engagement, apparently. The armies are described -- the French have three hundred and thirty-five thousand men but are outnumbered by the pagans who have at least one and a half million. This would represent a large proportion of the male population of Europe at that time.

"Clers fut li jurz e li soleilz luisanz" (3345), as is to be expected. Charlemagne encourages his men by reminding them of the death of Roland "l'altre soir" (3412). The battle continues until "passet li jurz, si turnet a la vespree" (3560). The pagans flee, and the French follow them to Saragossa which Charlemagne captures and where he spends the night, having had a very busy day: "passet li jurz, la noit est aserie" (3659). The next day -- "passet la noit, si apert le cler jor" (3675) -- Charlemagne sets off for home via an indirect route to Aix, where the death of Aude and the trial and execution of Ganelon take place. Night falls and Charlemagne dreams of a new task set for him by God: "'Deus,' dist li reis, 'si penuse est ma vie!'" (4000).

To work out a chronology of the events of the _Roland_ is clearly not possible, since all too frequently there is no indication of the duration of individual events, particularly journeys. The time between the events is not considered. Further problems which increase the difficulties are those connected with the identification of various places. Blancandrin leaves Marsile at "Sarraguce" and reaches the French at "Cordres" in an unspecified (but short) time, and the next day Ganelon returns with him, then after plotting with the pagans rejoins the French who are now at "Galne." If "Sarraguce" is, as universally accepted, Saragossa, is "Cordres" Cordova as Menéndez-Pidal thinks, or is it Cortes in northern Spain? Is "Galne" on the French or the Spanish side of the Pyrenees? Where are the French when they hear Roland sounding his horn? After Roland's death is avenged, the French sleep near the Ebro but the next day return to Roncevaux in time to bury the dead, defeat Baligant's army, and then take Saragossa. Many of the attempts at identification assume that the poet is trying to be realistic: "Cordres" cannot be Cordova because it would take weeks to get there from Saragossa -- therefore it must be Cortes that is meant. But if one is to be logical in this manner, how can one explain the other unrealistic details of the poem such as the exaggerated numbers of troops, to take an obvious example? Surely it is more sensible to assume that the place-names, as well as other "factual" details, are not used in a representational sense.

Journeys are essentially timeless, with one or two exceptions. For example, after Ganelon reaches the French

camp at Galne at dawn the army marches until nightfall.
But time spent in one place is more frequently specified --
after the Saracen embassy meets with Charlemagne, night falls
and in the early morning the emperor hears Mass and Matins;
a battle begins sometime in the day and lasts until the
evening.

This lack of continuous time agrees perfectly with the
sense of discontinuity mentioned in the quotations given at
the beginning of this section: each event takes place and is
described, then the next follows immediately, the time interval between them being ignored. Action fills the time
necessary for it, but time has no existence, no interest
aside from its connection with events. An analogy can be
made to a strip cartoon or, more appropriately perhaps, to
the Bayeux tapestry in which scenes are literally stitched
together, each scene being a unit which can stand by itself
although closely linked to those next to it. Even when
describing the events in the Roland or the Bayeux tapestry
it is extremely difficult to convey the impression each gives
without some kind of schematic representation, since we
today are from birth completely conditioned to thinking and
writing and visualizing in a continuous linear manner. To
try and account for time in the Roland is not only impossible,
but is totally foreign to the spirit of the poem.

Let us now look at another early poem of the heroic
tradition, the Old English Beowulf, which seems to occupy a
curious position in the oral-literary continuum. Albert Lord

firmly states that it is an oral-formulaic production, citing
several studies: "The documentation is complete, thorough,
and accurate. This exhaustive analysis is in itself sufficient
to prove that Beowulf was composed orally."[10] Scholes and
Kellogg agree, but suggest "a textual tradition of up to two
and a half centuries" before the manuscript we have came into
being. This seems contradictory, and there are certainly
those who do not agree with the idea that Beowulf was composed orally.[12] Donald Fry remarks, in a recent paper, that
"a consensus seems to be emerging that written Old English
poetry used oral forms, but no reliable test can differentiate
written forms from oral poems" and that "improvization remains a keystone of formulaic theory as well as one of its
major stumbling blocks: most modern critics find the subtleties
of Beowulf or Elene too profound for extemporizing."[13]
Klaeber refers to the poem's "stock of formulas ..., [its]
preliterate stage of poetry." But most critics agree with
Klaeber that the poem combines Christian and pagan characteristics: "Christian elements are deeply ingrained in the very
fabric of the poem" and "Germanic military ideals are still
clearly recognizable."[14] Perhaps a study of the concepts of
time in the poem will help to elucidate these questions.

Unlike the Roland, Beowulf begins with a reference to
the past: "we hear of the glory of the kings of Spear-Danes
in days gone by" -- "in gēardagum," of how Scyld Scefing used
to perform. His death and sea-burial are also clearly in the
past. Then comes the genealogy of Hrothgar and the building

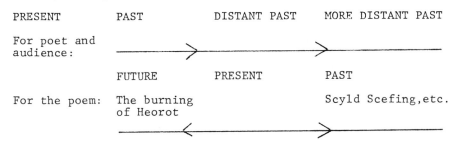

of Heorot. The fate of Heorot, to be burned, is expressed
as in the future -- "wæcnan scolde" -- but is still in the
past, obviously, for the poet and his audience. So we have
already a complicated time-scheme:

The past for the poet and his audience includes three elements
of "pastness" which are distinct, and then in the references
to the songs in the hall is added a fourth, since the poet in
Heorot sings of the Creation, how "se Ælmihtiga eorðan worhte"
(92). This is clearly as far back in time as one can go and
suggests a linear concept of time. But for the moment we
shall not consider the structure of the poem, but will concentrate on the chronology of the action, returning to the
digression in the next chapter.

Heorot is built, Grendel becomes enraged at the joyful
clamor in the hall and "syþðan niht becōm" (115) the monster
sets out on his first raid, killing thirty men. "Ða wæs on
ūhtan mid ærdæge" (126) that his terrible deed was discovered
-- in the darkness, just before dawn. No date or even season
is given for the beginning of Grendel's attacks, but we are
told that they continue for twelve years. During this time
many councils were held and various heathen practices indulged

in: "swylc wæs þēaw hyra, hæþenra hyht ... Metod hīe ne cūþon"
(178-80). This is an interesting passage since it sets up a
definite contrast between the present (Christian) audience
and the behavior of the men of the past, of the world in which
the action of the poem is taking place. This is an indication
of historical consciousness different from what one expects
in a preliterate culture.

One assumes that the period of twelve years referred
to is ended by Beowulf's setting out, though there is no
explicit logical connection: the poet does not say "twelve
years until one day Beowulf set forth." In fact, there is
an awkwardness of construction which makes it difficult to
decide the temporal relation of events: lines 135^b to 146^a
describe the second and subsequent raids, until "oð þæt īdel
stōd hūsa sēlest" (145-46). The raids continue for twelve
years -- although the hall is empty the killings do not stop.
Hrothgar takes council, seeks a plan. Are these three sections of the poem consecutive in time or are they concurrent?

Joan Blomfield has said that "the poet has detached
his theme from the process of time and space and disregarded
the appearances which for practical purposes constitute
reality."[15] Let us see if this is true for the actions of
the hero in the main narrative. Beowulf sets out for Heorot
in an unspecified season and ends his journey across the sea
"ymb āntīd ōþres dōgores" (219), the meaning of which is not
exactly clear; Clark-Hall has "in due time on the second day,"
but Klaeber's note suggests "after the normal lapse of time

on the following day" but says that one might understand it
as meaning "one day and as much as is necessary of another"
(Klaeber, p. 137). Since we have no idea what time the hero
departed, to say that he reached Hrothgar's country "on the
second day" is about as precise as can be. Klaeber adds,
"whether the distance from Beowulf's home to the coast near
Hleiðr could really have been covered in so short a time, is
to be doubted." This last comment reveals the same kind of
concern with "reality" that we have already talked about in
relation to the Roland.

Beowulf and his men are greeted by the coastguard and
sent on their way; they reach Heorot and are led in to Hrothgar where a great deal of conversation takes place before
and during dinner. We may assume, perhaps, that the Geats
get to Heorot sometime in the afternoon of the second day.
Then "sunu Healfdenes sēcean wolde/ æfenræste" (645-46), the
Geats are left in charge of Heorot and, except Beowulf, fall
asleep. Grendel, of course, "cōm on wænre niht" (702), and
the battle with Beowulf ensues. The only indication of time
here is the comment after Grendel's defaet that Beowulf
"nihtweorc gefeh" (827), but this does not necessarily mean
the fight lasted all night, just that it occurred at night.
This is the end of the second day.

"Ða wæs on morgen" (837), the third day begins. Some
men track Grendel to the mere in which he died and on the
return one of them composes a praise-poem for Beowulf. Presumably, "on morgen" refers to the early morning since as

the men race home the sun rises: "Ða wæs morgenlēoht scofen ond scynded" (917-18). Heorot is decorated and a celebratory feast is held which begins at the appropriate time: "Ða wæs sǣl ond mǣl" (1008). The feast continues, with many ominous digressions, until Hrothgar retires "syþðan ǣfen cwōm" (1235).

In Beowulf's absence, Grendel's mother attacks and carries off Æschere sometime during the night; at daybreak -- "ǣrdæge" (1311) -- Beowulf meets with the king in council. They track Grendel's dam to the lake, taking no measured time for the journey. Beowulf arms himself and dives down into the lake. We are now in the fourth day. The descent to the bottom of the lake occurs in the daytime -- "hwīl dæges" (1495)[16] -- and the battle with Grendel's mother lasts an unmeasured period. The lake boils with blood, however, and Hrothgar and the watching Danes assume the worst and leave "Ða cōm nōn dæges" (1600), which Klaeber glosses as 3 p.m. But since, as we have shown, the medieval canonical hours are variable according to the season "the ninth hour" would be a better gloss -- as long as it is understood that the hour in question does not represent a precise sixty minutes. If we assumed, for example, the events to have taken place in early June, the ninth hour would be about 4:30 p.m. GMT.[17]

An unspecified time later -- "sōna" (1618) -- Beowulf swims to the surface with his trophies and then with his companions returns to Heorot to report his adventure. The inevitable speeches and banquet follow, and as night falls the old king retires, as does the hero shortly after. This is the end of the fourth day.

The raven announces sunrise -- "heofenes wynne" (1801) -- which chases away the shadows, and the Geats prepare to return home. Beowulf and his men leave with their treasure and sail home uneventfully. If we assume -- though there is no real reason why we should since sailing conditions vary so much -- that the return voyage tales the same amount of time as the outward one, the Geats' whole adventure lasts less than one week. They arrive home in the late afternoon as "sigel suŏan fūs" (1966) -- the sun was hastening from the south. At the banquet, Beowulf tells Hygelac and the assembled Geats the story of Grendel and his mother, accounting for the three days of the action but omitting his final night at Heorot and the journeys to and from Hrothgar's court.

The dragon episode begins after an indeterminate time during which Hygelac has been killed and Beowulf has taken the throne and ruled for "fīftig wintra" (2209), until the dragon-hoard, undisturbed for "þrēo hund wintra" (2278) is robbed and the dragon comes into action. Like Grendel, this is a night creature: it waits impatiently "oŏ ŏæt æfen cwōm" (2303) before it begins its attacks and flies back to its barrow "ær dæges hwīle" (2320) -- before daytime.

We are told that Beowulf and the dragon are to die at the same moment -- here there is no suspense about the outcome of the struggle, in constrast to the Grendel episode. Beowulf has survived various battles until this particular day arrives:

"oð ðone ānne dæg" (2399). This day is significant because
of the events which occur during it. No time of day is
indicated as the hero and his men set out. One assumes it
is daylight so that they can see what they are doing and so
that they are sure to find the dragon at home.

Beowulf kills the dragon with Wiglaf's help but himself
is mortally wounded. The news is carried to the stronghold
and all come to view the corpses. The funeral takes place
and the poem comes to an end. The whole action of the dragon
episode seems to have occupied only a single day.

We can see, I think, that a chronology for Beowulf --
even though an imprecise one -- can be worked out: probably
six days for the first half of the poem and less than one for
the second half, with a gap of more than "fīftig wintra"
between them. In this respect the poem differs from the
Roland in which any attempt at a chronology is quite impossible. There is also in Beowulf a perspective on time which
is lacking in the Roland: many references to past and future
time (from the poem's viewpoint) and different degrees of
pastness from the viewpoint of the poet and his audience.
Most remote is the Creation, mentioned several times, then
the genealogy of Scyld Scefing and that of Beowulf which
brings us to the time of the poem. Digressions of various
kinds refer forwards and backwards in relation to the time
of the poem, but are all past for the poet and his audience.
There is, then, a linear sense of time, an historical sense
-- though imprecise -- which one would not expect in an

orally composed poem. Contrary to Blomfield, quoted above (p. 49), the poet has not totally "detached his theme from the process of time and space."

Let us now look at some Old Icelandic poetry, from the poetic Edda, for comparative purposes. The poems, Atlakviða and Atlamál are shorter than either Beowulf or Roland but are different from each other in interesting ways.

Atlakviða is generally accepted as a tenth century poem, but whether early or late is debateable.[18] The poem is composed in the Germanic alliterative line divided by modern editors into stanzas usually of eight four-to-six syllable lines, each pair of which is connected by alliteration.

The chronology of the poem, even though the events are much less difficult to follow than those of the Roland, is impossible to work out. There is not a single time-reference in the entire poem, not even a mention of sunrise or sunset, although stanza thirty has "sól inni suðrhǫllo" -- the southward-curving sun -- which may indicate morning.

The poet assumes his audience knows the characters of his narrative since there are no introductory remarks: "Atli sendi ár til Gunnars" ('Atli sent a messenger to Gunnarr' [1]); no mention of place, rank, relationships, or time (except simply the past) is made at first.

The messenger, Knefroðr, arrives with an invitation to Gunnarr and his brother to visit Atli. Inducements are offered (and despised) and the question of acceptance is debated. Atli's wife is Guðrún, sister to the two brothers.

She has sent the hair of a wolf twisted in a ring and it is
this warning of danger which spurs the Nibelung brothers to
ride to the Huns: it is a challenge they cannot refuse.

Gunnarr and Hǫgni must ride across "Myrkvið inn ókunna"
('Mirkwood the unknown') and pass all Hunmark. One assumes
a great distance is covered before "land sá þeir Atla" ('they
see the land of Atli' [14/1]), but no mention of any kind
is made of the duration of their journey nor of the time of
day of their arrival or departure.

Guðrún meets and warns them, but it is too late and
the brothers are seized. First a slave's heart and then
Hǫgni's are brought to Gunnarr who defies his enemies' efforts
to exhort the secret of the family treasure from him. He is
led out to die in a snake-pit. After Gunnarr is dead, the
Huns return to the hall where Guðrún helps serve a feast --
a dish of her and Atli's sons. One presumes the Huns ate in
the evening since after the horrific revelations of cannibalism, Atli goes to bed where Guðrún kills him and burns down
the hall. It is possible, however, that the brothers arrived
in the morning, were disposed of before lunch, and that Atli
was accustomed to taking a nap early in the afternoon. But
we have absolutely no way of knowing -- and to ask questions
such as "how long would it take to cross Mirkwood; how long
would it take for Gunnarr to die of his snake-bites; how
long would it take for Guðrún to prepare the meal?" are irrelevant, foreign to the concepts of the poem, as we concluded earlier with reference to similar questions concerning
the Roland.

For a new reader, the poem contains considerable tension. As Ursula Dronke says, "the poem is ordered in three great acts, and each act is given its own climax: each moves from doubt to certainty, from concealment to revelation" (p. 13). Will Gunnarr and Hǫgni accept the invitation in spite of their sister's warning? Once at Atli's fortress, will they escape death? After the killing of her brothers, what form will Guðrún's vengeance take? The pace of the narrative, which contains not a single moment of rest, carries the reader (or listener) along with it.

The poem is set in the unspecified past and as the poet seems to assume a knowledge of the characters they would appear to be part of the traditions of the audience; the poem would then belong in what Erich Auerbach, discussing Homer, refers to as a "uniformly illuminated, uniformly objective present."[19]

Atlamál in Grœnlensko tells essentially the same story as does Atlakviða but the approach is different. Atlamál is more than twice as long (one hundred and three stanzas instead of forty-four) and seems to be a combination of several different sources. The version it most resembles is that of Þidrek's Saga, which is of the thirteenth century, but it is set in Jutland and has resemblances stylistically to the Icelandic family sagas. From this and other evidence, Dronke suggests that it is a written poem from Greenland, of the twelfth century (p. 111).

Other characteristics of the kind we have been discussing

would seem to suggest a written origin -- the poem is more
"realistic," less "mythic," and pays a little more attention
to time. But let us consider the chronology of the poem.

Compared with Atlakviða, the setting is more clearly
in the past -- "þá er endr" ('long ago') -- as the poem begins.
There was a meeting, which Guðrún overheard, at which Atli's
plot was laid. Atli's messengers, along with the invitation,
carried a warning from Guðrún cut in runes. No time indication is given here. There is a feast after which Hǫgni and
his wife Kostbera prepare for bed. Kostbera reads the message: "kunni hon skil runa" ('she knew the meaning of the
runes' [9/2], which apparently few did). She dreams an
ominous dream which she tells Hǫgni who misinterprets it.
Gunnarr and Glaomvǫr awake and similarly the husband ignores
the wife's dreams. When it is light ("er lýsti" [27/1]),
they get up and the men leave for Atli's place. Their voyage
across the sound takes some time -- "litlo ok lengra" (36/1)
-- and they reach Atli's farm. There is no mythic ride
across Mirkwood and all Hunmark. Guðrún joins her brothers
and their three companions and the battle begins. It lasts
most of the day: "Morgin mest vágo, unz miðian dag líddi,
ótto alla ok ǫndurðan dag ('they fought most of the morning
until midday was past, all of the early morning and beginning
of the day' [50/1-4]). The Nibelungs are defeated, finally,
but the death of the brothers is almost an anti-climax to
the deaths in Atlakviða; here the emphasis is on the fighting.
It seems that they were kept prisoner overnight before their

executions, since "dags var heldr snemma" ('it was rather early in the day' [64/2]) when they died, and "morginn er nu" ('it is morning now' [65/5]) Atli tells Guðrún. Guðrún appears to submit to his power and suggests they have a memorial feast, to which Atli agrees.

The time taken for the feast to be prepared is not given, though if we agree with Dronke that "lagat var drykkio" (73/2) means 'the drink was brewed', there must have been a delay of several weeks (p. 134). But is seems more likely that the phrase merely means 'the drink was prepared'.

Guðrún's slaughter of her children and the transformation of their skulls to drinking-vessels must have occurred before the feast, so stanzas seventy-four and seventy-five, which describe this scene, must be a flashback. As Guðrún begins to tell Atli of her deeds -- after the eating and drinking -- she mentions that he had told her it was morning when her brothers were killed, a reference back to stanza sixty-five. "Man ek enn þann gerva" ('I remember that clearly' [78/6]), she says, and "nú er ok aptann" ('now it is evening' [77/7]). The implication is a comparison between morning then and evening now, and there is a question of her remembering details so it would seem that a considerable time has passed, though there is no way of knowing how much.

Atli and Guðrún threaten each other with death and Guðrún jeers him and implies that something will happen to him before the next morning -- "ár morgin" (84/6). The poet here brings in Hniflungr, Hǫgni's son, whom we have not met before; he was not in the original group that came to Atli's farm. He and Guðrún kill Atli who, while dying, takes part in a bitter exchange with Guðrún about the past. Guðrún promises Atli a decent burial whereupon he dies.

No further time indications are given, and no chronology of the poem can be constructed. There is more of a sense of time in this poem than in Atlakviða, however; there is a feeling of the past, and of the past as being different from the present (as in the last dialogue between Atli and Guðrún) which is quite absent from the shorter poem. These differences could certainly be connected to a difference in literacy of the tradition of the poem.

Regarding these four early poems solely from the point of view of chronology of the action, what kinds of comments can we make? The Roland, although it is the longest of our examples and although it contains many words and phrases connected with time, has little concern with the division of time into linear sections which can be joined in a continuum, an account of time. The day comes and the action begins; the day ends and so do the events. When there is more action, another day is filled with it. Atlakviða consists of nothing but action, but this is totally unrelated in any way to the passage of time, and no chronology is possible. Time scarcely exists even in the most simple way; there is not a reference to any of the cycles of Nature. With Atlamál no chronology can be worked out, but, like Roland, it includes some references to the changes of the natural world. Also like the

Roland, there are references to the world of writing -- the
message from Guðrún is a written one, as are the messages
from the pagans to Charlemagne and back. But none of these
poems is organized in any temporal sense as we would understand it. Beowulf, however, in spite of the complexity of
its narrative structure, has a central core of action which
is clearly organized in a chronological manner -- perhaps
it is not as precise as we might wish, but nevertheless a
discernable time-scheme exists.

In the next chapter we shall discuss some later medieval
works of definite literary composition, beginning with Yvain,
one of Chrétien de Troyes' romances. We shall enter a different world of time.

NOTES

[1] Evan Hadingham, Circles and Standing Stones (New York: Doubleday, 1976); Gerald S. Hawkins, Stonehenge Decoded (London: Fontana, 1970); Alexander Marshack, The Roots of Civilization (New York: McGraw Hill, 1972).

[2] Michael Ventris and John Chadwick, The Decipherment of Linear B (Cambridge: Cambridge University Press, 1958).

[3] Eugene Vinaver, The Rise of Romance, p. 10.

[4] W. P. Ker, Epic and Romance, p. 290.

[5] Erich Auerbach, Mimesis, p. 100.

[6] Ibid., p. 95.

[7] J. J. Duggan, The Song of Roland: Formulaic Style and Poetic Craft.

[8] P. Boissonnade, De Nouveau sur La Chanson de Roland (Paris: Champion, 1923), p. 128.

[9] Ramón Menéndez-Pidal, quoted in Paul Aebisher, Rolandiana et Oliveriana (Geneva: Droz, 1968), p. 244.

[10] Albert B. Lord, The Singer of Tales, p. 198.

[11] Robert Scholes and Robert Kellogg, The Nature of Narrative (New York: Oxford University Press, 1966), p. 34.

[12] For example, Larry D. Benson, "The Literary Character of Anglo-Saxon Formulaic Verse," PMLA, 81:334-41.

[13] Donald K. Fry, "Caedmon as a Formulaic Poet," in J. J. Duggan, ed., Oral Literature: Seven Essays, pp. 1,5.

[14] Fr. Klaeber, Beowulf and the Fight at Finnsburg (Boston: D. C. Heath & Co., 1950), pp. lxvi, xliv, lxii.

[15]Joan Blomfield, "The Style and Structure of Beowulf," in Donald K. Fry, ed., The Beowulf Poet (Englewood Cliffs, New Jersey: Prentice-Hall, 1968).

[16]At the latitude of Copenhagen (56N), sunrise on July 1, 1975 was at approximately 3 a.m., sunset at 9 p.m. This means that each of the twelve canonical "hours" will be about ninety minutes. "None" would therefore be at about 4:30 p.m. At the time of the action of the poem, there would have been some variation from these figures. Source: "Local mean time of sunrise and the beginning of astronomical twilight -- meridian of Greenwich," in American Ephermis and Nautical Almanac (Washington, D.C.: United States Printing Office, 1976).

[17]Ursula Dronke, The Poetic Edda, Vol. 1, Heroic Poems (Oxford: Clarendon, 1969), pp. 42-45.

[18]Auerbach, Mimesis, p. 5.

Chapter III

ACCOUNTING FOR TIME: LATER TEXTS

I should now like to move to some later medieval narratives, in which we shall find ourselves on more familiar
ground regarding time. We shall begin with Le Chevalier au
Lion (Yvain) of Chrétien de Troyes.[1]

Immediately one is struck by two differences from the
Roland, the first of which is the form of the poem. Instead
of stanzas or laisses linked by assonance, each of which with
few exceptions describes a single incident, we see a continuous narrative of rhyming couplets which at once gives an
impression of linearity. Secondly, Yvain is set firmly in
the ideal past while the author of the Roland solicits the
audience's complicity in the timeless epic present: "Carles
li reis nostre emperere magnes..." (Roland, line 1; emphasis
added). At the court of King Arthur they talk of love and

> li deciple de son covant,
>
> qui lors estoit molt dolz et buens;
>
> mes or i a molt po des suens...
>
> or est Amors tornee a fable
>
> Mes or parlons de cez qui furent
>
> si leissons cex qui ancor durent
>
> (16-29)

The past is explicity contrasted with the present -- to the
disadvantage of the latter -- and the poet says that the
name of King Arthur will last forever. There is thus clearly
a linear idea of time connecting past, present, and future,

and a sense of the past as different from the present. There is nothing like this in the Roland.

Yvain begins at a fixed point -- the feast of Pentecost -- which gives a precise point of departure for the story, whereas in the Roland we are merely told, after an introductory laisse, that Marsile is at Saragossa with no indication of the date or even season. Almost at once Chrétien takes us further into the past as Calogrenant tells the story of his adventures which took place seven years previously. After having travelled a thorny road in seach of adventures for an unspecified time, Calogrenant arrived at a castle where he was welcomed and stayed the night. In the morning, "lors que l'en pot le jor veoir" (268), he left the castle and almost at once met the keeper of the bulls who told him of the mysterious fountain and put him on the right road. Calogrenant reached his destination just before noon: "Espoir si fu tierce passee / et pot estre pres de midi" (410-11). He poured water on the stone, the storm broke, the birds then sang, the knight rode up, and the duel took place. The events follow each other rapidly, in a linear manner. After his defeat, Calogrenant rested awile considering what to do next, then took off his armor and walked crestfallen back to the castle where he had spent the previous night. He arrived "la nuit" (561) at the castle and received a courteous welcome. The story is completed "Ensi alai, ensi reving; / au revoir por fol me ting" (577-78), and we return to the feast at King Arthur's court.

Yvain responds to the story by promising to avenge Calogrenant, while Kay, with his jeers, asks Yvain if he will leave that same day or the next and adds that if he has bad dreams in the night he can always change his mind. The king hears the story from the queen and is delighted by it. He swears to go to the fountain within fifteen days; "ja einz ne passeroit quinzaine" (666), and sets the date by referring to the feast of St. John the Baptist, which is always celebrated on June 24th; Pentecost is therefore June 9th. The time-period should be kept in mind since it defines precisely the action of the first part of the poem -- Yvain's journey to the fountain, his defeat of Esclados le Roux, his falling in love with the lady, his courtship, marriage, and the arrival of Arthur's court. Yvain is unhappy at the king's plan as he wants the adventure for himself. The future tense is used here to express his intention and his expectations: "il ne les atendra ... ira ... querra ... trouverra" (691-98). He is impatient to act, and this impatience adds to a tension lacking in the Roland. A date has been set before which Yvain has to accomplish his adventure.

Yvain swears to himself to find Calogrenant's mysterious fountain in the forest of Broceliande "jusqu'a tierz jor" (696) -- with no directions from Calogrenant apparently -- and after travelling over enormous distances finds the thorny path leading to the castle. The next morning he sets out for the fountain, defeats Esclados, follows him back to his castle, and is befriended by Lunete who tells her story in a

brief flash-back (1004-1025) and gives him a ring of invisi-
bility. Yvain falls in love with the lady of the castle whom
he sees attending the funeral of her husband Esclados, and
Lunete promises to help him. Lunete tries to calm her lady
and promises to find a better husband than Esclados -- a
defender of the fountain is necessary since they have already
heard that King Arthur is on his way: "Li rois Artus i vendra /
qui doit venir l'autre semainne" (1620-21). The news has
come by letter from a friend at the court.

Presuming that Yvain did in fact reach the forest in
three days, on the morning of the fourth he set out for the
magic fountain and it is now the evening of that day, June
13th. By drawing attention to the imminent arrival of the
king, Chrétien heightens the readers' expectations and increases the tension in a rather modern way which does not
surprise us, but seems to have been a new technique.

Lunete points out to her mistress that none of the local
knights are worth anything and suggests that the man who
killed Esclados was the better man. The lady is, naturally
enough, extremely angry and sends her confidante away. During
the night, however, she becomes anxious about the protection
of her fountain (1736-39): the reader also wonders whether
Reason will conquer Emotion. The lady, in a typical example
of Chrétien's technique, debates with herself the rights and
wrongs of her husband's death and her duty regarding his
killer, and ends by convincing herself that she does not hate
the man who killed her husband.[2]

In the morning Lunete reappears and the lady asks her
the practical questions concerning name, rank, and lineage
which one needs to ask about a prospective husband. The
answers prove satisfactory, and the lady wants to see him at
once: "quant le porrons nos avoir?" (1822). 'In five days'
she is told, but she protests that this is too long. 'I want
him to arrive tonight or tomorrow.' Lunete says that even a
bird could not go and come back in such a short time: a
messenger will be sent who will reach Arthur's court the next
evening. "Cist termes est trop lons assez: / li jor sont
lonc," (1834-35) she responds. Since the moon is up, the
messenger can cover two days' journey in only one, the lady
suggests, and if he does he will be suitably rewarded. Lunete,
in the face of her lady's impatience, promises that she will
have Yvain "antre vos mains" in only three days -- "jusqu'a
tierz jor" (1846).

This whole scene uses time to produce tension and
expectation -- looking forward to what the future may bring
-- involving the reader in the action in a way not attempted
in the _Roland_ in which the scenes unroll successively with
an inevitability which has previosuly been mentioned.

Since, in fact, Yvain is already at the castle, the
period of five days at first suggested by Lunete is almost
arbitrary -- linked in a realistic way to the distance to
Arthur's castle certainly, but reducible to three days without too much difficulty. According to our previous discussion
Yvain himself took between three and four days for the journey

but he, of course, had to find the way. Chrétien is showing
us, through the dialogue with Lunete, the ardor of the lady
of the castle, and is testing her passion for the reader to
see.

Duting the next three days, Yvain is bathed, his hair
is washed and dressed (1883 ff), he is robed in fine clothes,
then presented to the lady. He humbles himself before her
and in a charming scene their peace is made. Yvain is then
brought before the people of the castle and the chamberlain
outlines the situation: King Arthur is descending upon them
"ençois que la quinzainne past" (2087). He refers to the
lady's previous marriage and to the custom of the fountain
which has lasted for "plus de .lx. ans" (1206).

Her knights encourage the lady to marry without delay,
for, they say, "molt est fos qui se demore / de son preu
feire une seule ore" (2137-38): 'He is very mad who delays
acheiving his goal for a single hour.' So the marriage is
solemnized the very same day. Chrétien tells us that now
that Yvain is the lord, the dead man is completely forgotten.
Past events are no longer significant -- one must think of the
future.

The wedding celebration lasts "jusqu'a la voille / que
li rois vint a la mervoille" (2173-74), that is, a not inappropriate seven days. The time-scheme has been accurately
worked out with no awkward gaps, and the passage of time has
been used to increase the reader's interest.

Yvain successfully defends the fountain against Kay and

invites the king and his court to stay, which invitation is accepted for "huit jorz antiers" (2310). Everyone passes the week in great rejoicing: "a grant joie out le tans usé / trestote la semainne antiere" (2468). Gawain persuades Yvain to ask leave to go with him to the tournaments to gain honor for himself and his lady.

Laudine grants him leave, but with precise limits after which her love will turn to hate: he must return in "un an / huit jorz aprés la Saint Johan / c'ui an cest jor sont les huitaves" (2575-77). That is, exactly one year from the day, since it is now the eighth day of the feast of St. John which began when Arthur arrived. It is, therefore, July 1st.

Yvain departs, leaving his heart behind him, to follow the tournaments with Gawain, "et li anz passe tot voie" (2674). They are so involved with their exploits that "tot li anz fu trespasses / et de tot l'autre encor assez / tant que a la mi aost vint" (2678-81). The middle of August is about six weeks after Yvain should have made his way back to his wife Laudine -- the passage of an entire year occupies five lines only. Yvain is engrossed in his pursuit of renown and appears to take no notice of the passing of time. One might expect him to have been reminded of his promise by the feast of St. John, which should have been celebrated wherever he was, but the implication is that he was too busy even to keep the feast days. The significance of this six weeks -- excessive as it seems -- is not clear. As Yvain sits by the king he begins to think of Laudine and realizes that he has broken his word: "covant manti li avoit / et trespassez estoit li termes" (2702-04). At this moment, as if summoned by his despair, a girl appears on horseback and reveals Yvain's perfidy to the whole court, using extremely insulting terms: "mancongier," "guileor," "desleal," "tricheor," and so on (2721-22). The promise is enunciated: "Tu devoies revenir / a ma dame jusqu'a un an; / jusqu'a la feste saint Jehan / te dona ele de respit" (2750-53). This seems to contradict lines 2575-76, which spoke of "un an huit jorz apres la Saint Johan," but it is likely that, like the canonical hours, a feast may refer to a duration of time as well as to a point in time -- a week or "huitaves."

We are told that Laudine has some system of keeping record of the passage of time in her room -- a calendar of some kind, perhaps -- since "en sa chambre poinz a / trestoz les jorz et toz les tans / ... tote nuit conte et asome ... les jorz qui vienent et qui vont" (2756; 2759; 2771). She is clearly a numerate lady concerned, as would be a modern heroine, with counting off the days until her lover returns.

The young lady, after upbraiding Yvain for nearly fifty lines, seizes her mistress' ring from Yvain's finger and departs, leaving Yvain struck dumb.

During Yvain's subsequent period of madness in the forest the passing of time is not noted. We are only told that not a week goes by without Yvain leaving an animal he has killed for the hermit, who, in turn, puts bread and water out for him. We have no way of being certain of the duration

of Yvain's insanity but may perhaps assume at least several
weeks. He is discovered "un jor" (2884) by two "dameisles"
and their lady, by whom he is recognized, healed, taken care
of, and told that he needs "un quinzainne" to recover his
health (3078).

From this moment, presumably in the autumn, begins the
recovery of his good name. During these adventures, there
is occasionally more than one event taking place at the same
time, and there may also be a conflict between episodes so
that the question arises as to whether Yvain will reach a
certain place before it is too late. Instead of merely
seeking for personal glory, Yvain now asks if he is needed:
"Or me dites donc / se vos avez besoing de moi?" (3074-75).
He has fully recovered his strength when Count Alier comes
on "un mardi" to attack the lady of Norison with whom he is
staying. There is no indication before, during, or after the
battle of the intervals of time involved. In spite of the
lady's pleas, Yvain leaves as soon as the treaty is drawn up
with the defeated count.

Yvain's next adventure, that of the lion, begins at
once. He rescues the lion from an attacking dragon and they
become companions, the lion hunting game for both of them.
They follow this simple life for a fortnight until by chance
they find themselves at the magic fountain where, after he
recovers from his swoon, Yvain laments his failings and is
overheard by the imprisoned Lunete whom he then is able to
repay for her past help by promising to defend her. Tension

is created here by the imminence of danger: "Demain serai
ceanz prise / et livree a mortel juïse" (3589-90). She adds
that Gawain and Yvain are the only two who could defend her
although her situation is Yvain's fault: "por cui demain
serai a tort / livree a martire de mort" (3620-22). No
reference is made to the time at which she is condemned to
die, although later Yvain says that his appointment to protect
her is for "demain a ore de midi" (3844).

Here there is a conflict of chronologies: we have already
seen that Yvain's insanity began in mid-August and it logically
lasted for several weeks since not a week went by that he did
not leave some game for the hermit. Yvain needs a couple of
weeks to ragain his strength before he defeats Count Alier and
then he spends a fortnight travelling with his lion before he
reaches the magic spring and the imprisoned Lunete. Allowing
only a month of insanity, the date must be somewhere in mid-
October.

Lunete tells Yvain, however, that she was given a time
limit of "trente jorz" (3685) to find a champion to defend her,
and that the time is up the following day. We are not told
when her trial for treachery took place expect that it was
"quant ç'avint que vos eüstes / l'an trespassé que vos deüstes /
revenir a ma dame" (3655-57), but even if this was not until
mid-August (when Yvain realized his failure), it is clear that
much more than thirty days has elapsed since the onset of
Yvain's recovery. Here, clearly, Chrétien nods.

After promising to help Lunete, Yvain finds shelter at

a local castle where the people are suffering from the
deprivations of the giant Harpin de la Montagne whose latest
demands must be met by the following midday: "Einz que midis
soit" (3823). When Yvain hears the story he promises to be
of assistance if he can, but adds that he hopes that the
giant will arrive early as he himself must be "aillors que
ci / demain a ore de midi" (3943-44). As we have just seen,
there was no specified time mentioned by Lunete but in spite
of this omission Chrétien uses the conflict of schedules to
produce anxiety in his characters -- and in his readers.
Yvain repeats that nothing in the world will prevent him from
keeping his previous promise to be: "demain a midi ... au
plus grant afeire por voir / que je onques poïsse avoir"
(3990-92).

In the morning the tension mounts as after Mass Yvain
waits "jusqu'a prime" (4027), then tells his host that he
must be on his way. He delays only after he is beseeched in
the names of the Holy Family to stay. Chrétien dwells on
Yvain's agony of indecision, then relieves it by having Harpin
appear soon enough for the hero to dispatch him and take leave
of the grateful family. Yvain again mentions that he has an
important engagement: "car einz que midis soit passes / avrai
aillors a feire assez / se je i puis venir a ore" (4295-96).
The last line translates as 'if I can get there in time.'
Chrétien does not let the tension slacken as he tells us that
already, with Yvain riding as fast as his horse can carry him,
Lunete has been brought to the stake: "mes ainz que il poïst

venir / a la chapele, en fu fors treite / la dameisele, et la
rez faite / ... trestote nue en sa chemise" (4312-14; 4316).
Will the hero reach the damsel in time?

The villains who accused Lunete are dragging her, bound,
to the fire while Yvain struggles towards her through the
crowd, delayed as he is by the sight of his wife who is looking
on but does not know his identity. Chrétien keeps us in
suspense for fifty lines before Yvain gest close enough to
speak to Lunete who is on her knees having just gone to con-
fession. The battle takes place, Yvain and his lion defeat
the three accusers, and after a poignant conversation with
Laudine, Yvain rides off carrying his wounded lion on his
shield. He rides until he comes to a castle by which time
it is, naturally, time to rest: "Est tans de herbergier"
(4668). They stay here for an indefinite period, until the
lion is better: "Jorz i sejorna ne sai quanz" says Chrétien
(4694). This phrase gives a delicate touch of versimilitude
to the story -- as if Chrétien had actually heard the story
himself.

There are some interesting -- though vague -- time-
references toward the beginning of the next adventure, that
of the daughters of the lord of Noire Espine. The younger
sister, seeking help, arrives at Arthur's court "s'voit tierz
jor que la reïne / est de la prison renenue / or Meleaganz
l'a tenue" (4735-36). This is a reference to the story of
Le Chevalier de la Charrete (Lancelot), another of Chrétien's
romances which concerns the love of Lancelot and Guinivere.

It will be recalled that when Lunete went to the court for
help, she found Gawain absent in search of the queen who had
been abducted. The time which has elapsed between Lunete's
appeal to the king and the appeal of the daughter of Noire Espine
appears to be about the same as that taken by the whole
action of Lancelot.

The news of Yvain's defeat of the giant Harpin has arrived at court on the same day (4740-45), but from this point
on it becomes impossible to reconcile all the implications of
the passage of time.

The daughter of Noire Espine is given fourteen days to
find a champion (Yvain), and travels through "mainte contree"
(4814) looking for him. She hears no news, falls ill, and
is looked after by friends whom she tells of her quest. While
she is recovering, another girl takes her place in the search
for Yvain, who finds herself benighted at the castle where
Yvain had arrived "avant ier" (4901) and had killed the giant
Harpin. The reader expects that a great deal of time has
elapsed since the daughter of Noire Espine left the court --
she travelled to many places, fell ill, and her friend has
also been searching. But we are told that the corpse of
Harpin is still not buried: "Demain porroiz veoir le cors /
d'un grant jaiant" (4908-09), the lord of the castle tells
his guest. Since Yvain arrived in the evening and killed the
giant the next morning, the battle must have occurred only
the day before the girl reached the castle. The following
morning she is directed to the magic fountain and meets Lunete

who rides with her in the direction Yvain had taken. The
girl seeking Yvain continues until she finds "la meison ou
mes sire Yvains / ot esté tant que tot fut sains" (5003-04).
But he has just left -- she can catch up to him if she does
not delay: "Mes gardez vos de trop tarder" (5018), and she
does, in fact, overtake him.

Since it is now only two days since Harpin was killed,
the time apparently taken for Yvain and his lion to recover
from their wounds can only be, logically, two nights and the
intervening day. This is the period of which Chrétien said
"jorz i sejorna ne sai quanz" (4694). The time which the
daughter of Noire Espine spent in travelling through "mainte
contree" and getting sick with worry should therefore be re-
duced to only one day even assuming that the news of Harpin's
death reached Arthur's court at once. I think we must agree,
therefore, that in this part of the narrative we cannot account
for time in any reasonable manner. The duration of events is
occasionally clear though often vague, but the interval between
events is not considered. This is different from the way the
same problem is treated (or rather not treated) in the Roland,
since in Yvain relative time intervals are mentioned in words
such as "avant ier" and "demain."

Yvain and the girl ride along together after he has
agreed to defend the daughter of Noire Espine. As night falls
they reach the castle of Pesme Aventure which they enter in
spite of cries of "mal veigniez, sire, mal veigniez" (5109).
Inside the castle there are three hundred girls in a sweat-

shop atmosphere whose story Yvain and the girl hear before
meeting the lord of the castle and his family, from whom they
receive a proper welcome. After a good dinner Yvain retires
to bed with his lion at his feet.

At dawn, Yvain gets up, hears mass and then kills the
two demons; he releases the girls, refuses the offer of the
lord's land and daughter, and again continues his travels.
He wanders for a week -- "trestotz les jorz de la semainne"
(5807) -- before returning to the lady of Noire Espine who
quickly recovers after being sick for a long time: "malade
et gëu longuement," we are told. The king is at the castle
where he had been for a "quinzainne ou plus" (5838), and the
fortnight he allowed the lady to find her champion has almost
ended: "N'il n'i avoit que un seul jor / de la quinzainne a
parvenir" (5852-53). The case will be settled before the day
is over.

Yvain and his party spend the night away from the castle
but as dawn breaks and it becomes full day they prepare for
the judgment. Gawain has been away also, but he is lodged
nearby and also gets ready. The days seem to pass almost un-
noticed -- the knights arise at dawn, and Gawain at least has
a specified distance to cover (three or four leagues) to reach
the court: this appears to take him several hours, for as soon
as he approaches the court the elder sister speaks, suggesting
that time is up. "Sire, ore passe, / jusqu'a po sera none
basse, / et li derriens jorz iert hui" (5883-85). "None," as
we have already seen, is the mid-afternoon hour, and the

period which ends the afternoon, that is from about 4 p.m. to 7 p.m. in the summer. "None basse" refers to the time just before "none," and according to custom the waiting period is not over until "none" in past -- but whether this means the point of time or the period of time is not clear.[3] In any case, the elder sister is a little hasty in her jubilation. For the modern reader there is considerable tension here, but on this occasion Chrétien does not make the most of it.

The king tells her to wait until he has actually given his judgment because there is still time: "Ancor vendra trestot a tans / vostre suer ci, si con je pans" (5911-12), and, of course, at that very moment Yvain and the younger sister arrive. The elder refuses to settle the dispute, and the duel begins. After a long digression concerning the friendship of Gawain and Yvain and the conflict in which they are involved, Chrétien returns to the battle with neither knight gaining an advantage. They fight so long that "li jorz vers la nuit se tret" (6199) and the combatants rest. "La nuit ... vient oscure" (6214) and after both knights compliment each other, they identify themselves, the king settles their disagreement, the gives his judgment in the legal case and all is well.

As soon as Yvain has recovered from his wounds, he sets off in search of the magic fountain and causes a storm which threatens Laudine's castle with destruction. The castle, of course, is now without a defender, and as Yvain waits at the fountain Laudine and Lunete discuss the situation. Lunete

suggests that the knight of the lion is the man they need and
that is return for his help they should help him regain the
good graces of his lady. Laudine swears to do this and Lunete
sets off to find Yvain. She is surprised to find him so soon:
"Ele ne cuidoit pas / trover a si petit de pas" (6657-58).
Yvain, Lunete, and the lion join Laudine at her castle where
the reconciliation between the husband and wife takes place.

In Yvain, in many situations time depends on the action
-- it is the events which determine the passage of time and
not vice versa. The duel between Gawain and Yvain is a case
in point: the coming of night is a convenient way for Chrétien
to achieve what he needs to achieve, the inconclusive end of
the battle. Therefore, night falls. The sequence of events
is not usually determined by any logic of time, but each event
is determined by the one which precedes it: in the dispute of
the sisters of Noire Espine, King Arthur says that the younger
sister, he thinks, will arrive in time, and as he says this
she appears as if conjured out of the air by his thought.

Time is occasionally used to produce tension in a modern
way but opportunities which might be taken by a post-Renais-
sance author are ignored by Chrétien. In the earlier part of
the poem, as we have pointed out, Chrétien accounts for time
in an interestingly consistent way. He is conscious enough
of time so that he can use it as a literary device, but this
consciousness is not so much a part of his mental being that
he has to account for time. His attitude seems to be intermediate between the disregard for time of the Roland and the

dominant role of time in later literature.

The plot of Chrétien's Yvain depends very much on time,
in that the hero's insanity and search for rehabilitation are
direct results of his forgetting the date of his promised
return home. In the fourteenth century Middle English poem
Sir Gawain and the Green Knight[4] the plot is even more closely
related to a similar promise -- a promise which in this case
is kept in the foreground of the hero's (and the reader's)
consciousness; the narrative describes Gawain's unrelenting
efforts to keep the appointment he made.

Morton Bloomfield, in an article summarizing the work
on Sir Gawain and the Green Knight up until 1960,[5] makes some
interesting remarks on time in the poem:

> Cyclic time or the time of nature is superimposed
> on linear time or the time of history in order to
> contrast the two and to point up Gawain's dilemma.
> The winter to some is not merely the same as last
> winter, but different.

This contrast between cyclic and linear time has not been
used in any of the poems we have so far considered, even if
it has been implied, and the conscious skill with which it is
manipulated in Sir Gawain and the Green Knight shows a consistent awareness of time which is new to us -- time informs
the whole structure of the narrative.

Like the poems of Chrétien, Sir Gawain and the Green
Knight is clearly set in the past at Arthur's court, but here
we are also given the preceding history of Britain:

> Siþen þe sege and þe assaut watz sesed at Troye ...

Fro riche Romulus to Rome ricchis hym swyþe...

And fer ouer þe French flod Felix Brutus

On many bonkkes ful brode Bretayn he settez

(1, 8, 13, 14)

The poet is telling us, in his present, what happened in "þat ilk tyme ... as I haf herde telle" (24, 26). We are in the linear time of history and the past is deliberately contrasted with the present.

Since the tension of the poem depends largely on punctuality, we should expect the poet to account for time carefully, and this he does -- with one apparent error where there seems to be a missing line which we shall discuss later.

The action of the poem begins at the court during a season of feasting: "þis kyng lay at Camylot upon Krystmasse ... ful fiftene dayes" (37, 44), to be precise on New Year's Day: "Wyle Nw 3ere watz so 3ep þat hit watz nwe cummen" (60).

Dinner is served but the King will not eat until something wonderful happens -- "sum aunturus þyng an uncouthe tale ... sum mayn meruayle" (93-4) -- and as he converses with his noble knights before the laden dinner table the Green Knight clatters into the hall. The challenge is given, as a "Crystemass gomen" (284), for one of the company to give a blow and receive one in return after a "twelmonyth and a day" (298)[6], a usual time interval in such stories. Gawain severs the Green Knight's head with one blow, the stranger picks it up and after admonishing Gawain to keep his promise, rides away. The rest of the day is spent in pleasure -- "wyth wele walt þat þat day" (485).

At the beginning of the next section, the poet emphasizes the changes that take place from one year to the next: "A ȝere ȝernes ful ȝerne, and ȝekdez never lyke, / þe forme to þe fynisment foldez ful selden" (498-99). He then describes the cycle of the seasons in general terms which imply repetition of a similar sequence: "After Crystenmass com þe crabbed lentoun ..." (502) then in springtime "flowerez þere schewen ..." (507) followed by "þe softe somer þat sues þerafter" (510). "Bot þen hyȝes heruest" (521) after which "al grayes þe gres þat grene watz ere ... and wynter wyndez aȝayn" (527, 530). Here we have a juxtaposition of linear and cyclic time to which we have referred above -- one year is never the same as the next nor does the end match its beginning, but the seasons follow inexorably the same repeated pattern.

About the feast of Michaelmass -- the end of September -- Gawain begins to think of his "anious vyage" (535), although his encounter is still three months in the future. He stays with Arthur, however, through October until All Saints' Day, November 1st, when he asks permission to leave: "I am boun to þe bur barely to-morne / To seche þe gome of þe grene" (458-59). He remains for the rest of the day and prepares himself "on þe morne" (566), that is, on November 2nd he "gaf þem alle goud day [and] wende for euermore" (668-69).

The geography of Gawain's voyage is not agreed upon, but the poet appears to know the route from a southern area

through North Wales to the Wirral near Chester. No reason
is given for Gawain to go north, but the color green is often
associated with the Devil in Medieval England, and the dwelling
of the Evil One was traditionally in the North.[7]

The time Gawain takes to reach his goal is not charted
in detail by the poet, but the journey is eventful and the
distance covered is considerable as well as within the bounds
of possibility.

> Mony klyf he ouerclomn in contrayez straunge...
>
> at vche warpe ... he fonde a foo...
>
> So mony meruayl ... þe mon fyndez...
>
> Sumwhyle wyth wormez he werres...whyth wolues...
>
> wyth wodwos ... wyth bulles and beres, and borez...
>
> And etaynez ...
>
> (713-23)

We are told that "he frayned, as he ferde, at frekez þat he
met, if þay hade herde any karpe of a kny3t grene" (703-04),
but all of them "nykked hym wyth nay" (706).

Gawain himself was carefully keeping track of time since
he knows when "Krystnasse euen" (734) has come and prays to
Mary for guidance that morning. As he prays for a place to
rest and to observe the holy day, he sees a castle which he
approaches and is invited to enter. The treatment of the
journey is different from that of the eponymous hero in Yvain
-- we have seen already that Chrétien is not concerned with
filling in the gap between important events either with
activities or with a reference to the passage of time.

Gawain is made welcome, meets the lord of the castle and is led to dinner, which, although it is sumptuous, is described as "þis penaunce" (897) since no meat is served. Christmas Eve is a fast day before the great holiday of Christmas Day itself. When dinner is over, "hit watz neȝ at þe niyȝt þe tyme" (928), and vespers is heard at which Gawain meets the ladies of the castle. The wine is served at the fireside "til þat hit watz tyme" (991) and they all retire to bed. There is here a timely ordering of events.

"On þe morne" (995), Christmas Day, there is feasting and music which continues on "þat day and þat oþer, and þe þryd ... þe ioye of sayn Jonez day ... þe last of þe layk" (1020-23). The third day, the feast of Saint John, is December 27th, but the editors agree[8] that a line must have been omitted here since the three temptations and the three hunts clearly take place on the last three days of the year, and, as Norman Davis remarks "the author is attentive to dates" (p. 104).

The guests begin to leave "when hit watz late" (1027) and Gawain also wishes to go but his host detains him and asks what can have taken him from the king's court at that season. Gawain tells the lord of his quest and that although he does not know how to find the place he seeks, he would not fail to reach it "on Nw ȝeres morne for alle þe londe inwyth Longres" (1054-55). He explains his errand, says that he now has "both þre dayes" (1065) to accomplish it, and repeats the strength of his intention -- he would rather die than fail. The date is therefore December 28th and the time is evening.

His host tells Gawain that he will show him the way to the green chapel; Gawain need only "ferk on þe fyrst of þe 3ere and cum to þat merk at mydmorn ... dowellez whyle New 3eres daye ... hit is not two myle henne" (1072-78). The distance to the chapel is defined in time -- less than half a morning's ride -- as well as in miles.

Gawain cheerfully agrees to stay until New Year's morning, and accepts the suggestion that he stay and rest in the castle while the lord goes hunting. The exchange of winnings is agreed upon and after some more talk all go to bed.

The people of the castle rise early to prepare for the hunt and hurry to Mass and then to the woods "by þat any dayly3t lemed upon erþe" (1137). Hunting of the deer lasts all day, "to þe derk ny3t" (1177).

While this clamorous activity continues outside, the lady of the castle makes her first attempt at the seduction of Gawain in his bedroom; their conversation goes on "til mydmorn paste" (1281) and after Gawain dresses and hears Mass, they "made myry al day, til þe mone rysed" (1313). The lord, with his people, returns "bi þat þe dayly3t watz done" (1365), the exchange of winnings takes place, and after dinner they retire to bed having agreed to renew their pledge.

The next day follows a similar pattern in which the time is filled with activities from before dawn until after dusk: before "þe coke hade crowen ... bit þryse" (1412) the lord and his men are up and off to the woods "er any day sprenged" (1415) where they follow a "wylde swyn til þe sunne schafted" (1467), "whyle oure luflych lede lys in his bedde" (1469).

The lady again tempts Gawain and the couple "laȝed and layked longe" (1554). After she leaves him, he "ryses to þe masse" (1558), dines, and enjoys the company of the ladies all day while the lord hunts. No time is specified for their reunion at the end of the day, but one may assume it was late afternoon since the hunt went on until "þe sunne schafted" (1467), that is, the sun was setting. After dinner and wine by the fire, the exchange of winnings takes place and Gawain asks permission to leave, but his host swears he will be able to reach his goal if he leaves on "Nw ȝeres lyȝt, long bifore pryme" (1675). They agree to repeat their agreement "on Nw ȝeres euen" (1669), and the lord emphasizes that the day is the second in the series of three -- "for I haf fraysted þe twys" (1679) -- so the date must be December 30th. The same pattern if repeated as on the preceding days:

> Sir Gawain lis and slepes
>
> Ful stille and softe al niȝt;
>
> Þe lord þat his craftez kepes,
>
> Ful erly he watz diȝt
>
> (1686-89)

Again, the huntsmen are out before dawn since they see "vpon rak rises þe sunne" (1695). The fox leads them a dance until "myd-ouer-vnder" (1730) -- the middle of the afternoon.[9]

Gawain is visited by the lady, from whom, after much urging,
he accepts the magic girdle. He gets up, receives absolution
at the castle chapel, and as usual "he mace hym mery among
þe fre ladyes ... to þe derk ny3t" (1885-87). The lord
begins his return home when "hit watz nei3 ny3t" (1922), and
the usual festivities take place in the castle. At bedtime,
Gawain takes his leave, since he had to depart early: "I mot
nedes, as 3e wot, meue tomorne ... to dele in Nw 3eres day
þe dome of my wyrdes" (1965-68).

The poet begins the next section dramatically: "Now
ne3ez þe Nw 3ere and þe ny3t passez" (1998). Gawain lies
half awake and "bi vch kok þat crue he knwe wel þe steuen"
(2008). He dresses "et þe day sprenged, / For þere watz ly3t
of a laumpe þat lemed in his chambre" (2009-10). Gawain
leaves the castle when it is light enough to see that "Vch
hille hade a hatte, a myst-hakel hugh" (2081), but it is not
until some distance had been covered is it the "sesoun þat
þe sunne ryses" (2085). His guide warns Gawain of the danger
he faces but Gawain resists the suggestion that he flee and
finds the green chapel -- a mysterious place indeed, as
Gawain comments: "Here my3t about mydny3t þe dele his matynes
telle! (2188-89). To reverse the usual sequence of Hours has
become evil indeed! Time has become part of the sacred order
of things.

The Green Knight sppears and praises Gawain for his
punctuality:

Þou hatz tymed þi trauayl as truee mon schulde

And þou knowez þe couenauntez kest vus betwene

And I schulde at þis Nwe 3ere 3eply þe quyte

(2241-44)

This praise is certainly well deserved since Gawain had no
precise name or address to go by, nor was the transportation
system of those days as reliable as might be desired.

Gawain endures the three axe-blows, refuses an invitation to return to the castle, and travels back to Arthur's
court, having various adventures on the way -- as before,
the time of his journey is not specified but is full of events:

Wylde wayez in þe worlde Wowen now rydez...

Ofte he herbered in house and ofte al þeroute,

And mony aventure in vale ...

(2479-83)

In contrast to the opening of the poem, we are not given here
any indication of the time of day or even the season of
Gawain's return to the court, but the poet again makes clear
that the events he has been describing took place in another
time:

Þus in Arthurus day þis aunter bitidde,

Þe Brutus bokez þerof beres wyttenesse ...

After þe sege and þe asaute watz sesed at Troye

(2523, 2525)

"Brutus bokez," also referred to as "þe best boke of romaunce,"
might indicate any chronicles or romances of British times,
not necessarily connected to Brutus, as Davis points out (p. 131).

In this poem, written two hundred years after Chrétien, the attitude to time which we saw developing in Yvain -- the consideration of time as linear, and the interest in completing temporal sequences -- has become more consistent. There are no places in the poem in which the narrative leaps from one event to another, separated temporally from it as if there is an instantaneous transition. Journeys, even if not given time limits, are seen in geographical space and their temporal space is not left devoid of action.

The narrative unfolds, after the "historical" setting is given, during the Christmas season, on New Year's Day. After the challenge is offered and accepted, the cycle of the year is described; Gawain's preparations for his journey begin in the fall, his departure takes place on November 2nd, the dates being marked by the religious festivals of Michaelmas and All Hallows. Gawain reaches Bertilak's castle on Christmas Eve, and the duration of his stay -- until the early morning of January 1st -- is carefully accounted for (with the exception of December 28th which we have already discussed). His journey home, although not measured in time, is eventful. There are no points in the poem at which a modern reader might ask himself a question about the sequence of events nor is there any problem concerning duration.

Evidence of formulaic analysis[10] suggests that Sir Gawain and the Green Knight is an extremely literary production.

In Yvain the action as a whole moves forward -- the line may not be a direct one, but although there are diversions

from the straight and narrow, the movement is generally linear.
The author of Sir Gawain and the Green Knight, however, as
Bloomfield points out, uses both linear and cyclic concepts:

> The timeless but deeply segmented present as
> revealed in the cycle of the year is firmly
> embedded in the vaguely known past. Time
> functions as a part of the decorum and re-
> straint of the poem [but] this decorous, calm,
> and aristocratic world is menaced by the in-
> decorous, wondrous, and mysterious.... We
> [finally] return to the stability time per-
> spective can give.

Other scholars have commented on the tension between the worlds
of civility and savagery in the poem, between the oasis of
calm within doors and the harshness of nature without: the
Green Knight / Sir Bertilak threatens the one and subdues the
other. The time of history linear time, is closely connected
to the civilized world, to order and discipline, while cyclic
time is seen in the inexorable and repeated changes of the
seasons. "Natural" time, uncivilized, unlettered time, is
cyclic; artificial, literary time is linear. The separation
of Man from Nature, of literate from illiterate -- which T. S.
Eliot referred to as the "dissociation of sensibility" which
he saw developing in the seventeenth century, perhaps begins
here.

I shall now consider one of the Icelandic "Family Sagas,"
Gunnlaugs Saga Ormstungu, [11] probably written down about half-
way between the time of Chrétien and that of Sir Gawain and
the Green Knight, in te late thirteenth century.

The question of Icelandic saga origins is an interesting
and complicated one since many sagas contain and concern known

historical figues and events. Should they be taken as history
or as fiction? I think it probable that most scholars would
now agree that the answer is somewhere in between -- that the
narratives are based on a combination of written and oral
sources, with historical and fictional elements.[12] Compari-
sons between various texts reveal discrepancies not easily
explained by a completely written tradition but agreements
with historical facts which one would not expect in purely
oral compositions.

The setting of many of these narratives and of the one
we are considering, is Iceland, England, Norway, and Sweden
about the turn of the first millenium -- from the 980's to
the early years of the eleventh century. The earliest manuscript of Gunnlaugs Saga is mid-fourteenth century but the
date of composition is thought to be late thirteenth.[13]

As with Yvain and Sir Gawain and the Green Knight, the
crisis of the narrative depends upon the keeping of an appointment, although the terms of the agreement in Gunnlaugs Saga
and its interpretation are far less precise than in the case
in either of those poems.

The saga begins, as is traditional in the genre, with
the placing of one of the main characters in terms of kinship,
time, and space:

> Þorsteinn hét maðr; han var Egillson, Skalla-Gríms
> sonar, Kveld-Úlfs sonar hersis ór Nóregi; en Ás-
> gerðr hét móðir Þorsteins ok var Bjarnardóttir.
> Þorsteinn bjó at Borg í Borgarfirði; ... Hann átti

Jófríði Gunnarsdóttur Hlífar sonar. Hana hafði

átt fyrr Þóroddr, sonr Tungu-Odds, ok þeira

dóttir Húgerðr.

(51-52)

There was a man called Thorstein; he was the son

of Egil Skallagrimsson, the son of Kveld-Ulf, a

lord from Norway; Thorstein's mother was Asgerd,

the daughter of Bjarn. Thorstein lived at Borg

in the Borgar firths; ... He married Jofrid, the

daughter of Gunnarr the son of Hlif. She had

previously married Thorodd, the son of Tungu-Odd,

and their daughter was Hungerd.

Thorstein's genealogy goes back to his grandfather. His wife's

relations and her first marriage are mentioned as is the place

where they live, and Thorstein's physical appearance is

described. Although dates are not specified, enough well-

known figures from Icelandic history are referred to so that

the listener can place the story both temporally and socially.

The narrator situates himself outside the action as the

story begins, imprecisely enough: "Eitt sumar er þat sagt ...

('One summer, it is said...' [52]). A Norwegian, Bergfinn,

stays with Thorstein through the winter, then "um várit einn

dag" ('one day in spring') the two men go to work on Thorstein's

assembly-booth where later Thorstein has his prophetic dream.

Thorstein dislikes Bergfinn's interpretation of the dream but

takes it seriously enough to act upon it -- he tells his wife

to expose the child she is carrying if it turns out to be a

girl. The narrator at this point makes clear in a paren-
thetical statement that in his own (Christian) time the
practice of infanticide was not acceptable, but "er land var
allt at heiðt, at þeir menn, er félitlir varú ... létu út
bera bǫrn sin, ok þótti þó illa gǫrt ávallt" ('When the land
was all heathen, there were men who had little property ...
who exposed their children, but this was always thought a
bad thing to do' [56]). This is one of several points at
which it is obvious that the temporal setting of the story
is different from that of the narrator -- there is a historical sense of change. The clearest contrast is between the
pagan customs of former times and the narrator's Christian
tradition.

Thorstein rides to the Assemby that same summer and
Jofrid gives birth to her daughter who is taken secretly away
to be fostered by tenants of Thorstein's sister. "Nú liðu
svá sex vetr" ('Six winters pass like this' [57]) we are
told, until the child's identity is revealed and she is
brought back by Thorstein to his home.

We are now introduced to Gunnlaug "Serpent-tongue" and
his family. They were living "þenna tíma ... á Gilsbakka"
('at that time ... at Gilsbakki' [58]). When Gunnlaug is
"tólf vetra gamall" ('twelve years old' [59]), he quarrels
with his father Illugi and goes to Thorstein's where he stays
for a year. Illugi's daughter, Helga, and Gunnlaug become
friends: "Þau váru mjǫk jafnaldrar" ('They were about the
same age' [60]), so both are about thirteen years old.

Gunnlaug's eventual rival for Helga, Hrafn Ǫnundarson,
is now brought into the story with his relatives, and the
author makes an effort at historicity by linking the narrative to a great event -- the conversion of Iceland to
Christianity, which took place in the year 1000 AD. We are
also told that all the people who have been mentioned were
living at this same time: "Ok þessir menn, er nú eru nefndir,
váru allir uppi á einn tíma. ...ok þessu naer ... at landit
varð allt kristit" ('And these men, who have just been named,
were all living at the same time. ...And this was ... when
the country became completely Christian' [62]).

Although in this section I am only considering the ways
in which time is accounted for in Gunnlaugs Saga, I should
like to comment very briefly on the "historical" attitide of
the authors of Yvain, Sir Gawain and the Green Knight, and
Gunnlaugs Saga: in the first two narratives, the setting is
that of Arthurian Romance -- in the past, certainly, but it
is the idealized, unreal past. The author of Gunnlaugs Saga,
however, uses a setting which we know to be factual even if
some of the references are occasionally not precisely accurate -- after all, the events he mentions are more than two
hundred years before the date at which the text was composed.
We are inclined, it seems to me, to take the Icelandic text
more seriously as a reflection of historical fact.

One of Hrafn's relatives mentioned in the passage is
Skapti, "er þá var logsogumaðr" ('who was then lawspeaker'),
but in fact Skapti did not become lawspeaker until the year

1004, while Christianization took place in 1000 AD, so there
is a discrepancy here as far as dates are concerned although
the text uses rather vague time-expressions.

Gunnlaug has been living partly at home and partly at
Borg with Thorstein for six years since he first left his
father, "ok var hann þá átján ('and he was then eighteen
years old' [62]). He asks his father again to set him up
for a trading voyage and Illugi agrees, but Gunnlaug spends
much of his time talking with Helga at Borg and then asks
Thorstein to give him her hand in marriage. Thorstein, as
well as Gunnlaug's own father, is unhappy about the young
man's fickle behavior, but an agreement is made that Helga
shall wait for "þrjá vetra" ('three years' [67]) during which
time Gunnlaug must go abroad and make something of himself.[14]
We are given no indication of the season at this point nor of
the duration of the journey to Norway which Gunnlaug undertakes almost at once. We must bear in mind that the span of
time in this story is much greater than that in either of the
Arthurian romances we have considered so that the periods of
duration with which we are concerned are that much greater --
it would be unlikely that the author of such a story should
take account of short time-periods at this stage of his tale.
So far, we have heard about Helga's birth and the first six
years of her life, about Gunnlaug's quarrel with his father
at the age of twelve, his stay with Thorstein for one year,
and that he and Helga were of much the same age -- at that
point in the story, about thirteen. Then for six more years

Gunnlaug lives partly with one family and partly with the other before the plan to go abroad and the agreement for a three year delay in the marriage plans. All this is perfectly straightforward and is chronologically acceptable.

Gunnlaug's stay at the Norwegian court is extremely brief -- he barely escapes with his life, and the king, when he is told that the Icelander is eighteen, predicts that he will not see another eighteen years. In the autumn, Gunnlaug reaches London where he becomes attached to the court of King Ethelred (the Unready) who ruled from 978-1016 with an interval from 1013-14 when he was deposed by Svein Forkbeard. The first winter away from Iceland, Gunnlaug earns some fame in London by killing a dangerous berserk, but in the winter he asks permission to continue his travels and crosses to Dublin in the spring, presents King Sigtrygg with a poem, and after staying there a short time leaves for the Orkneys. Again he presents a poem to the local ruler, is rewarded, and continues his journey to Norway where in the autumn he reaches Konunga- hella. He presents a poem to the ruler of Skara, Earl Sigurd, and is invited to stay for the winter which he does. This is the second winter away from Iceland. During the Yule feasting, messengers come from Earl Eirik of Norway and Gunnlaug com- poses a poem which, when reported back to Eirik, helps to restore Gunnlaug to the earl's favor.

We may assume that Gunnlaug's next journey, to the court of King Olaf of Sweden, is made in the spring since Gunnlaug reaches Uppsala "naer þingi þeira Svía um várit" ('near the time of the Swedish Spring Assembly' [79]). It is here that he meets Hrafn Ǫnundarson and their rivalry begins.

Hrafn leaves for home "um várit ... ok sigldi til Íslands um sumarit ... ok var hann heima þann vetr með fǫður sínum" ('in spring ... and sailed to Iceland in the summer ... and was home with his father that winter' [81]). This is third winter since Gunnlaug left Iceland, and the following summer at the Assembly Hrafn asks for Helga in marriage. Clearly, this a crucial scene in the saga, and the author makes the proceedings straightforward.

Hrafn asks his relative Skapti, the lawspeaker, for his support and Skapti replies: "Er hon eigi áðr heitkona Gunnlaugs ormstungu?" ('Is she not already the betrothed of Gunnlaug Serpent-tongue?' [81]). Hrafn answers: "Er eigi liðin sú stefna nú ... sem maelt var með þeim?" ('Is not the interval now passed ... that was agreed between them?'). They agree that the time has indeed run out, and with their followers they go to see Thorstrin and ask for Helga. "Hon er áðr heitkona Gunnlaugs," ('She is already Gunnlaug's betrothed') Thorstein tells them, and Skapti asks, "Eru nú eigi liðnir þrír vetr, et til váru nefndir með yðr?" ('But are not the three winters passed that were agreed between you?' [82]). Thorstein agrees that the time is up but says that Gunnlaug may still return before the summer is over. Both sides agree to discuss the matter further at the following Assembly.

Gunnlaug has not returned by the following summer -- four winters have now passed since he left home -- and Hrafn pleads his case with Thorstein who goes to see Gunnlaug's father Illugi: "Þykki þér ek lauss allra mála við Gunnlaug, son þinn?" ('Do you consider that I am free of all agreements with Gunnlaug, your son?') asks Thorstein, and Illugi agrees that the conditions have been met -- he has no idea when Gunnlaug might return. There is still some latitude given, however, since the arrangement is that Hrafn and Helga be married at "vetnáttum at Borg, ef Gunnlaugr koemi eigi út á því sumri, en Þorstein lauss allra mála við Hrafn, ef Gunnlaugr koemi" ('the winter nights at Borg, if Gunnlaugr does not come out this summer, and Thorstein is free of all agreements with Hrafn, if Gunnlaug does not come' [82]).

At this point it is abundantly clear that Gunnlaug has not kept his part of the original plan and that Hrafn is consequently within his rights to ask for Helga. The author leaves the situation unsettled, however, with the new arrangement just made, and takes us back in time to the point where Hrafn left for Iceland and shows us what had prevented Gunnlaug from returning.

Gunnlaug left Sweden the same summer that Hrafn did but went to London as he had promised to do and spent the winter there -- his third since leaving Iceland. He wished to leave for home the next spring which would have enabled him to reach the Assembly at the same time as Hrafn, but because of the threat of a Danish invasion King Ethelred denied him permission.[16] So Gunnlaug's fourth winter away was spent in England. The following summer was also quiet and he was

allowed to set off after midsummer, just at the time that the
arrangement was being made at the Assembly in Iceland concerning Hrafn and Helga. From England he had first to get to
Norway and had difficulty finding a ship to take him since
'it was late in the summer': "þat var sið sumars" (84). Time
is running out -- in fact has run out so far as he knows.
From his shipmate, Hallfred, Gunnlaug hears stories about
Hrafn and admits that he knows Hrafn's pursuit of Helga. The
tension now builds in the narrative since we already know
that Gunnlaug has been given until the end of the summer --
but does he know this? There seems to be no way he could
know the details since it is obvious that Hallfred does not.

The duration of the voyage is not given but the ship
reaches Iceland in the north "hálfum mánaði fyrir vetr" ('a
half month before winter' [85]). After a wrestling match in
which Gunnlaug dislocates his ankle, his opponent, Thord,
tells him that he may do no better with his next opponent.
Gunnlaug asks Thord what he means and Thord says, "Við Hrafn,
ef hann faer Helgu innar vaenu at vetrnóttum, ok var ek hjá
í sumar á alþingi, er þat résk" ('With Hrafn, if he marries
Helga the Fair at the winter nights; I was there at the
Assembly in summer when it was arranged' [86]).

Here is the problem: Gunnlaug now knows that the marriage of Hrafn and Helga is arranged for the "winter nights."
There is clearly a condition attached since Thord says "ef
hann faer Helgu" and since Gunnlaug reached port two weeks
before winter there is plenty of time for him to get to Borg

and stop the wedding. But the time, like Gunnlaug's ankle,
seems to be out of joint, since although Gunnlaug and Hallfred
appear to leave at once -- there is, after all, reason for
haste -- they do not reach Gilsbakki until "þat laugerkveld,
er þeir sátu at brúðlaupinu at Borg" ('that Saturday evening,
when they sat down to the wedding feast at Borg' [87]). In
other words, it is the first day of winter and Gunnlaug is
too late. He wishes to ride to Borg at once -- a distance of
more than fifty kilometers -- but is dissuaded. He could not
possibly arrive until the wedding feast was over and the
marriage no doubt consummated. His ankle, we are told, is
still extremely painful and this is given as an additional
reason, although it has not prevented him from riding the
much greater distance from his landing place. The excuse of
his ankle also contradicts what we were specifically told of
Gunnlaug's character at the beginning of the saga when he
arrived at the Norwegian court with a boil on his foot but
refused to limp because of it.

What has happened to the two weeks since Gunnlaug's
return? The fact that his ankle is still painful implies that
the journey from the north to Gilsbakki has only taken a few
days at most. There seems no way the author can escape
serious criticism here concerning his use of time -- and at
the climax of his story. This is curious, since as we have
seen, although there are problems with the relation of the
chronology of the narrative to historical fact, the author has
accounted for time quite well within the frame of the saga.

The sequence of events since Gunnlaug left Iceland is well worked out and the narrative tension is increased by the juxtaposition of Hrafn's and Gunnlaug's adventures.

A modern reader would have made much of the proximity of Gunnlaug's return to the wedding at Borg. Perhaps the hero would be given only a week for the journey -- his damaged ankle would then by much more significant, and the ride south, intercut with scenes of the preparations for the wedding, could be made extremely dramatic. As we have already seen in Yvain, Chrétien exploits a not dissimilar situation with great effect when he depicts Yvain's difficulties in coming to Lunete's aid before noon on the day of his duel with the giant.

We are given a brief description of the wedding at Borg, the bride looking downcast, and then almost at once we are told of another wedding, that of Helga's half-sister Hungerd, which is to take place after Yule.

Between Helga's wedding and that of Hungerd, Hrafn has a dream which reveals to Helga that Gunnlaug has come back. Helga consequently becomes so harsh to Hrafn that they return to Borg and she refuses Hrafn his conjugal rights. This must happen within a month or two of their wedding.

At Hungerd's wedding Gunnlaug and Helga meet and talk for a long time. Just before everyone goes home Gunnlaug almost rides Hrafn down but a fight is prevented by Illugi and Thorstein. The following summer at the Assembly, however, Gunnlaug issues a challenge to Hrafn which is accepted but the two are separated before any serious harm is done. The Assembly comes to a close with a decision that such duels be forbidden in the future.

The author tells us that this duel was, in fact, the last in Iceland and that the Assembly that year was very crowded, with numbers equalling those after the death of Njál and after the Heath killings. These references to other sagas gives a kind of authenticity to the story, if not historicity.

Some undetermined time later Gunnlaug is at home at Gilsbakki when Hrafn appears and issues a challenge that they should both leave Iceland the next summer and arrange to fight in Norway. Time indications are very imprecise: it is "einn morginn" ('one morning' [97]) when Hrafn walks in, Hrafn refers to their previous encounter as taking place "í sumar" ('in the summer' [98]) so by implication it is now past summer. Hrafn also suggests that they should leave Iceland "í sumar" (obviously 'next summer' here).

Hrafn prepares his ship and sails -- one must presume in the summer -- reaches Norway where he spends the winter at Thrandheim, hears nothing from Gunnlaug and spends a second winter nearby.

Now we move back to Gunnlaug who left Iceland later in the same season but only reached the Orkneys for the winter and spent the following summer raiding with Earl Sigurd. No reason is given for his apparent failure to travel to Norway that summer: it is possible that there were no ships available,

but we are not informed of that. Gunnlaug arrives at Earl
Erik's court for the winter but is forbidden to fight Hrafn
within the earl's jurisdiction. In the spring, Gunnlaug sets
off for Lifangr although Erik knows that Hrafn has already
left for Sweden. There is no motivation for the moves of
Hrafn which follow -- surely a definite meeting-place for the
duel will have been arranged before the two left Iceland?
Even in times of rapid communications few people would merely
say, in a situation of honor such as this, "Let's meet in
Norway next summer." And there seems to be no conceivable
reason for Hrafn to go to Sweden.

The author sets up his story to produce some uncertainty
and tension is his audience, however -- there is the excite-
ment of the chase:

Þann morgin hafði Hrafn farit þaðan ... er Gunn-

laugr kom þar um kveldit. Þaðan fór Gunnlaugr i

Veredal ok þar at kveldi jafnan, sem Hrafn hafði

áðr verit nóttina. Gunnlaugr ferr, til ... Sůlu

... ok hafði Hrafn þaðan farit um morgininn.

Gunnlagur ... fór þegar um nóttina; ok um morgininn

í sólarroð þá sá hvárir aðra.

(100)

That morning Hrafn had left there ... when Gunnlaug

arrived in the evening. Gunnlaug left there for

Veradal and always arrived in the evening where

Hrafn had stayed the night before. Gunnlaug went

on to ... Sula ... and Hrafn had left there in

the morning. Gunnlaug ... went on at once
through the night; and in the morning at sunrise they saw each other.

The fight, then, begins soon after sunrise, and after
it is all over and the dead have been seen to, Gunnlaug's
guides carry him "allt ofan í Lifangr; ok þar lá hann þrjár
naetr ... ok andaðisk síðan" ('all the way over to Lifange;
and he lay there three nights ... and then he died' []03]).

The same summer, before the news of the duel has
reached Iceland, both Illugi and Ǫnund have dreams in which
their sons appear to them telling of their deaths. The next
year at the Assembly Illugi demands compensation of Ǫnund
which is refused. In the autumn, Illugi attacks Ǫnund's
family "snimma morgins" ('early in the morning'), kills one
and injures another. Hermund, Gunnlaug's brother, kills
another of Ǫnund's relatives the next spring with no reprisals
from Ǫnund. 'Some time later' -- "er stundir liðu fram " --
Helga marries Thorkel Hallkelsson, has several children by
him, is taken ill, and dies while looking at the cloak which
Gunnlaug gave her, a present to him from King Ethelred. No
time indications are given for any of these last events, nor
is there any link, direct or indirect, with historical facts
or other sagas.

How does Gunnlaugs Saga account for time compared to
Yvain and Sir Gawain and the Green Knight? First of all, we
must remember that a much longer time is involved -- we hear
about the whole of Helga's life from before her birth, in

fact, to her death, but even if we only wish to consider the
narrative as far as the death of Gunnlaug we still have to
reckon on a period of twenty-four or tweny-five years. We
should not expect, then, that the days and weeks be noted as
they were in Sir Gawain and the Green Knight or Yvain, but
the fact is that time is accounted for, by seasons and years,
quite precisely within the narrative itself and generally in
a linear manner. But when we come to smaller units, less
accuracy is achieved -- the vital two weeks from Gunnlaug's
landing in the north to the wedding of Helga are completely
mishandled according to modern literary standards. How different this is from the care with which the authors of Yvain
and Sir Gawain and the Green Knight delineate the passing of
days and even hours at the climaxes of their respective works!
These differences can be explained in several ways: the author
was incompetent or his scribe (if he had one) made mistakes;
Icelanders, literate or not, took no account of time-periods
of less than a month -- after all, for time-reckoning purposes
the year was only divided into two seasons, summer and winter,
although 'spring' and 'autumn' were used to indicate times
for travel and other activities. But it seems to me more
likely that this lack of interest in precision regarding time,
this ignoring of the possibilities of producing expectation
in the audience, may well be connected to the attitudes of a
preliterate or transitional society -- one which was beginning
to acquire the more literary and literate concepts of time
through an increase in a knowledge of the works of writers

such as Chrétien, whose romances were translated from French
in the second quarter of the thirteenth century. This is not
many years before Gunnlaugs Saga is thought to have been set
down.

Chaucer's "The Shipman's Tale," [17] classified by folk-
lorists as "the lover's gift regained," begins by describing
the characters, their relationships, and geographical location.
No attempt is made to relate the events to any others either
historical or mythical: "A marchant whilom dwelled at Seint
Denys" (1) is all we are told. How is time accounted for in
this fourteenth century story, contemporary with Sir Gawain and
the Green Knight?

The merchant prepares for a business trip "on a day"
(53) to Bruges, and invites his friend John, the priest, to
come and stay beforehand for "a day or twey" (59). The priest
does so, riding out from Paris. On the morning of the third
day of the priest's visit, the merchant goes to his office on
arising to make up his accounts "and thus he sit til it was
passed pryme" (88). As we have already seen, "prime" is the
first canonical hour of daylight (in effect, sunrise), and
also the period of the three hours after this -- keeping in
mind that the duration of an "hour" varied according to the
time of the year. In any case, "passed pryme" would mean that
the morning was half gone.

We leave the merchant in his counting-house and are
told what the priest and the wife are doing: here Chaucer
handles simultaneity very comfortably. "Daun John was rysen

in the morwe also" (89) and walks in the garden where he meets
the wife. Their conversation ends with the wife asking for
a loan of "an hundred frankes" in exchange for which she will
allow the priest to do "right as yow list devise" (192). A
hearty embrace follws, and the priest checks the time by his
pocket sundial: "By my chilyndre it is pryme of day" (206).
The two sets of characters are brought together in time, and
while the husband is working on his figures, the wife is
making money on her own account.

The wife, impatient to dine, knocks on the office door:
"How longe tyme wol ye rekene and caste youre sommes, and
youre bookes, and youre thynges?" (216-17). Her husband
explains the complexities of business and exhorts her to take
care of the household while he is away, for "to Flaundres wol
I go to morwe at day" (238) he tells her. Hastily a Mass is
said, speedily the table is laid, and quickly they all begin
to dine. After dinner, the priest borrows a hundred franks
from the merchant, and then after a short time he rides back
to his abbey.

The next morning, as arranged, the merchant sets off
for Bruges "and there I lete hym dwelle" (306) Chaucer tells
us. His stay away from home will be a considerable one, for
the distance from Paris to Bruges is more than two hundred
miles. Almost as soon as the husband is out of the way --
"the Sonday next" -- John the priest arrives, greets the
wife, and after a very brief discussion "in myrthe al nyght
a bisy lyf they lede" (318). In the morning the priest

"rydeth hoom to his abbeye" (323).

No estimation of the time that the husband is away is made -- he merely returns, tells his wife that he needs to borrow some money and at once leaves for Paris where he meets the priest. He informs John of his business activities and says that he has to borrow more money, and the priest quickly tells him that he has already paid back his hundred franks to the wife. The merchant is again successful in his business and goes back home happy in the thought of his profits.

The wife welcomes her husband cheerfully and they spend a pleasant night together. The next morning the merchant complains that she should have told him that the priest had paid his debt, but the wife defends herself by saying that she thought that the money was a gift, freely given, and with some witty remarks by the shipman, the story ends.

Chaucer does not account for time with much precision in this story -- the weeks necessary for the merchant's journey to Bruges and back are not even mentioned -- but there are no puzzling gaps or inconsistencies in the time sequence. The narrative depends on careful timing of the movements of the various characters in a way we have not seen in the other texts we have considered. Time, here, is used for profit, as a measureable commodity, equated with money at least by implication, and through the skillful juggling of time every-one profits. The husband "nedes moste he wynne in that viage / A thousand frankes aboven al his costage" (370-71), the wife has gained "an hundred frankes," and the priest has scored off

both husband and wife in diffent senses. As is appropriate
in a story of the mercantile class, the accounting for time
is seen as part of everyday life -- all three characters are
aware of the passage of time: the merchant borrows and lends
money against time, the wife is conscious of meal-times, and
the priest carries with him a device which measures time,
however inaccurately. In this tale of Chaucer's, the concept
of time has become internalized by the characters in a way
which is new to us in our investigation.

With Yvain, time is beginning to be accounted for.
Chrétien meticulously dovetails two sets of events in the
early part of the poem. Moreover, he uses time to create
tension in his audience, and characters are seen to show
impatience -- a wish that time would pass more quickly. The
fourteenth century Sir Gawain and the Green Knight scrupu-
lously accounts for time in places where it is significant,
for example, in the anticipation and preparation of Gawain
for the appointment which he has kept in mind, and also in the
days Gawain spends with Sir Bertilak. Journeys, though not
described in detail, are eventful and within the time-frame
of the narrative. There are no gaps in the flow of time.
Gunnlaugs Saga consistently accounts for time over a long
period and there is accurate correlation between the time-
tables of Gunnlaug and Hrafn. But at the climax of the plot,
when the audience is concerned about Gunnlaug's journey back
to Borg, the author ignores the possibilities of the situation:
something that Chrétien and the author of Sir Gawain and the

Green Knight would not have done. Accounting for time is part of the basic structure of the society in "The Shipman's Tale." Time passes as something outside the control of men, independent of their acts, which nevertheless must be observed and measured as it passes.

[1]Les Romans de Chrétien de Troyes: IV: Le Chevalier Au Lion (Yvain), Mario Roques, ed., (Paris: Champion, 1974). (Hereafter Yvain). References will be to the line numbers of this edition.

[2]For an excellent discussion of Chrétien's style in Yvain, see Charles Muscatine, Chaucer and the French Tradition (Berkeley and Los Angeles: University of California Press, (1957), pp. 26-27 and 47-54.

[3]Marc Bloch, Feudal Society, p. 74, refers to an argument over whether the time had come for judgment to be delivered as to the default of one of the two duelers: "Only one champion puts in an appearance -- at dawn; at the ninth hour, which marks the end of the waiting peroid described by the custom, he requests that the failure of his adversary be placed on record .... But has the specific period really elapsed? The county judges deliberate, look at the sun and question the clerics ... by whose bells [the passing of the hours] is measured more or less acurately. Eventually the court pronounces firmly that the hour of 'none' is past." Bloch gives the reference to Gislebert of Mons, ed. Pertz, pp. 188-89. The year is 1188, contemporary with Chrétien. See also Howard Bloch, Medieval French Literature and Law, Berkeley and Los Angeles: University of California Press, 1977: "The Grand Coutumier of Normandy defines the terminus ad quem of combat with the appearance of the stars in the sky" (ms. p. 61, note 74). The Grand Coutumier is early thirteenth century. This rule is relevant to the duel

111

between Yvain and Gawain which is said to end when "la nuit

... vient oscure" (Yvain, 6214).

[4]Sir Gawain and the Green Knight, (eds.) J. R. R. Tolkien

and E. V. Gordon, 2nd Edition, (ed.) Norman Davis (Oxford:

Clarendon, 1968). References are to the line numbers of this

edition.

[5]Morton Bloomfield, "Sir Gawain and the Green Knight: An

Appraisal," PMLA, 76 (1961), 7-19.

[6]Sir Gawain and the Green Knight, p. 84, note in line 298.

[7]F. N. Robinson, The Works of Geoffrey Chaucer (Cambridge,

Mass.: The Riverside Press, 1961), p. 705, note on lines 1380

and 1413 of "The Friar's Tale." The color and home of the

Devil.

[8]Sir Gawain and the Green Knight, p. 104, note on line

1022.

[9]Sir Gawain and the Green Knight, p. 120, note on line

1730.

[10]J. J. Duggan, The Song of Roland: Formulaic Style and

Poetic Craft, p. 18.

[11]Gunnlaugs Saga Ormstungu, (eds.) Sigurður Nordal and

Guðni Jónsson, Íslenzk Fornrit, III Bindi, Borgfirðinga Sǫgur

(Reykjavík: Hið Íslenzka Fornritafélag, 1938). (Hereinafter

Gunnlaugs Saga). References are to page numbers of this

edition.

[12]See, for example, Theodore M. Anderson, The Problem of

Icelandic Saga Origins (New Haven: Yale University Press,

1964); Peter Hallberg, The Iceland Saga, (tr.) Paul Schach

(Lincoln, Nebraska: University of Nebraska Press, 1962);

Gabriel Turville-Petre, Origins of Icelandic Literature (Oxford: Clarendon, 1953); Knut Liestøl, The Origin of the Family Sagas (Cambridge, Mass.: Harvard University Press, 1930).

[13]For example, P. G. Foote, Gunnlaugs Saga Ormstungu London: Nelson, 1957), p. xxii.

[14]The ship in which Illugi buys a share for Gunnlaug is owned by Auðun festargram. The author of Gunnlaugs Saga mentioned that it was he who refused to take the killers of Kjartan Oláfsson aboard after the killing, "sem segir í Laxdœla sǫgu, ok varð þat þó síðar en þetta" ('as it is said in Laxdale Saga, but that was later than this' [64]). The death of Kjartan probably took place in 1003 (Foote, p. xxiii), and Auðun was lost at sea the same year, so our author is placing Gunnlaug's voyage earlier than 1003. But compare this with note 16 on King Ethelred's rule in England.

[15]This is a variable feast but it is sometime toward the end of October.

[16]We are told that Knútr Sveinsson ruled in Denmark at this time. His father, Svein Forkbeard, had conquered much of England and had, in fact, deposed Ethelred in 1013 but died the next year. The author tells us that Knútr is attacking England after his father's death. So the date should be between 1014 (when Svein died) and 1016 (when Ethelred died) and Knútr did become king of England. This chronology is almost ten years different from that using Auðun festargram's

death as the fixed point.

[17]F. N. Robinson, The Works of Geoffrey Chaucer, pp. 156-160.

Chapter IV

PATTERNS OF TIME AND NARRATIVE: EARLY TEXTS

As we have seen in the previous chapter, a linear
sequence of time, a chronology of events was extremely difficult or impossible to construct in the early texts we considered, even though there were references to various indications either of points in time (such as Feast days) or
natural periods of time (such as days and nights). In this
chapter, I shall examine the same texts but this time with
regard to the patterns of time and of narrative structure --
are recurrent periods of time (days, months, years) related
in any way to narrative patterns? I shall be particularly
concerned with the correspondances or contrasts of cyclic and
linear design.

The first text I shall consider is La Chanson de Roland.
I shall begin by examining the whole poem to determine its over-
all structure and then proceed to break it up into smaller
and smaller elements.

The poem has been regarded as consisting of three parts
by those who would eliminate the Baligant episode, and of
four or five parts by other scholars, the majority in favor
of the four part division.[1] Let us accept, as in fact we
already have, the poem as we have it in the Oxford manuscript,
that is, including the Baligant episode.

J. J. Duggan has elegantly demonstrated that the poem
as an oral presentation falls into four parts, each introduced
by a group of formulaic elements which he calls an "articulation

motif."[2] The poem was thus presented in four "sittings,"
each of which corresponds precisely to one of the four main
divisions, or themes in Rychner's terms:

> Theme I (vv. 1-702):   The plotting of treason.
>
> Theme II (vv. 703-2608):   The battle of Roncevaux
>   and the destruction of
>   Marsile's forces.
>
> Theme III (vv. 2609-3704): The episode of Baligant.
>
> Theme IV (vv. 3705-4001):   The trial and execution
>   of Ganelon.

The next smallest element in the poem is usually taken to
be, on the narrative level, the motif or standard scene, and on
the presentational level, the laisse (a series of verses united
by assonance) or a group of laisses.

I should like to suggest, however, that there are other
elements of narrative, longer than the laisse or group of
laisses representing the motif, but smaller than the theme, of
which the poem may be said to be composed. I shall try to
answer the question as to whether there is any relation between
these elements (which I shall call Acts) and the various expressions referring to the natural cycles of day and night
which are scattered throughout the poem. As we have seen in
the previous chapter, such phrases have little or no function
in the poem's logical chronology.

Each of the four themes is divided into blocks of narrative separated by journeys -- in the first two themes there
are four journeys or parts of journeys, in the third there

are eight and in the final theme there are two. I should like to suggest that these are functional links between logically connected groups of motifs and that they effect the transition from one important part of the action to another; they also have a temporal function. Let us look as these narrative patterns.

THEME 1   THE PLOT

          Laisse

Act I   1 - 6   Introduction; Marsile's Council; Embassy
                      prepared

             7   JOURNEY (Blancandrin to Charlemagne)

Act II   8 - 11   Blancandrin gives message; Charlemagne's
                      hospitality

        12 - 26 Charlemagne's Council; Ganelon's departure

        28 - 31 JOURNEY (Ganelon to Marsile)

Act III 32 - 52 Ganelon and Marsile confer; Embassy prepared

           53   JOURNEY (Charlemagne to Galne; Ganelon joins
                      him there

Act IV   54   Ganelon gives message; Charlemagne's accept-
                      ance; JOURNEY (Charlemagne to France)

THEME 2   The Battle of Roncevaux and the Pursuit of
                      Marsile

           55   JOURNEY (Charlemagne to Roncevaux continued)

ACT I   56 - 65 Charlemagne dreams; Council; Selection of
                      rearguard

	66 - 68	JOURNEY (Charlemagne to France; Marsile to Roncevaux)
ACT II	69 - 79	Saracens boast, prepare for battle
	80 - 90	Saracens seen; the horn scene; Exhortation and prayers
	91 - 95	Exhortations; Battle is joined; Saracens boast
	96 - 127	Main battle; Marsile's troops arrive
	128 - 135	Roland and Oliver, second horn scene; Roland blows horn, Charlemagne hears
	136 - 139	JOURNEY (Charlemagne's return)
ACT III	140 - 177	Roland returns to battle; Oliver and Roland; Oliver dies; Pagans flee; Roland dies
	178 - 179	JOURNEY (Charlemagne reaches Roncevaux, pursues pagans)
ACT IV	180 - 188	Time stops; Destruction of pagans; Charlemagne dreams; Marsile flees to Saragossa and faints

THEME 3 — The Baligant Episode

ACT I	189	Flashback; Baligant's preparations
	190 - 191	JOURNEY (Baligant's voyage to Saragossa)
ACT II	192 - 193	Baligant's council; Embassy to Marsile
	194	JOURNEY (messengers to Marsile)
ACT III	195 - 198	Messengers give message; Marsile's council
	199	JOURNEY (messengers to Baligant)
ACT IV	199 - 200	Messengers give news of Roncevaux; Baligant's decision to attack Charlemagne

	201	JOURNEY (Baligant to Marsile)
ACT V	202	Marsile surrenders power to Baligant
	203	JOURNEY (Charlemagne to Roncevaux)
ACT VI	204 - 213	Regrets; Burial of the dead
	214	JOURNEY (Baligant to Charlemagne)
ACT VII	214 - 263	Preparations; Battle; Death of Baligant and destruction of Saracens
	264	JOURNEY (Charlemagne's pursuit to Saragossa)
ACT VIII	265 - 266	Capture of Saragossa
	267	JOURNEY (Charlemagne to Aix)

THEME 4		Ganelon's Trial and Execution
	268	JOURNEY (Charlemagne to Aix, continued)
ACT I	269 - 270	Vigil and funeral of Aude; Ganelon's torture
	271	JOURNEY (vassals to Aix) St. Silvestre (December 31)
ACT II	272 - 291	Trial; Duel between Thierry and Pinabel; Ganelon's execution; Conversion of Bramomonde [JOURNEY necessary: Charlemagne to Imphe "Deus, si penuse est ma vie!"]

The preceding chart shows how the journeys contained in the narrative break it up into sections (or Acts) of varying lengths: some are of one or two laisses (particularly in the

third theme), while others are as long as sixty-five (Theme
2, Act II -- the battle of Roncevaux). Each Act, however, is a
self-contained sequence of action which itself is composed of
only a few or perhaps as many as fifty motifs developing and
ornamenting the particular Act.

In the previous chapter we quoted several scholars on the
discontinuity of the Roland's struture: W. P. Ker refers to "a
succession of separate scene with no gradation between them";
Gaston Paris to "une suite d'explosions successives"; Erich
Auerbach comments that the Roland "strings independent pictures
together like beads." But none of these remarks makes clear
precisely what the authors mean by a scene. I suggest that
the Acts into which the journeys divide the narrative can be
regarded as the "independent pictures," and the journeys frame
them, linking as well as separating them. If the Acts are the
beads, the the journeys are the string. The journeys are
necessary to the coherence of the whole, neutral themselves
but linking the scenes, each of which has its own brilliance
and significance but forms part of a larger though discontinuous design.

On this level of structure, then, the poem is arranged
paratactically -- the Acts succed each other with no logical
grammatical connections -- but the journeys join them together so that the movement is generally forward as regards
narrative development, though jerky: "une suite d'explosions
successives" is very apt. Each Act comprises a collection of
motifs on the narrative level and laisses on the structural

level.

Jean Rychner[3] discusses the structure of the Roland
but was not aware of the articulation motifs which, according
to Duggan, mark the divisions between the four themes, the
four sittings. Rychner marks the end of the first theme
("Prélude à Roncevaux") at laisse 68 after Roland has been
selected for the rearguard and Charlemagne moves off with
the main body of his army toward France. Rychner does not
end theme II ("Roncevaux") with laisse 185 (the pursuit of
Marsile's army) but adds laisses 202-212 (Charlemagne's return to Roncevaux and the burial of the dead). Theme III
("Baligant"), then, begins with laisses 186-201 which are
followed by the praparations for the second battle (laisses
214ff), and ends with the capture of Saragossa at laisse 266.
Theme IV ("La Jugement de Ganelon") continues from laisse
267 to the end.

Rychner's subdivision of each of the four themes occasionally matches mine since at several points he marks laisses as
transitional which are in fact journeys: e.g., laisse 7
(Blancandrin's journey to Charlemagne); 27 (Ganelon's departure); 68 (Charlemagne's departure for France); 138 (Charlemagne's return); 266 (Charlemagne's journey to Aix). On the
levels of motif and laisse, Rychner describes five ways in
which consecutive laisses are linked (emphasis added):

(1) enchaînement, which consists of the repetition at the
    beginning of one laisse of what was said at the end of
    the previous one:

1. 148 : 1982   'Deus,' dist li quens, 'or ne sai jo que

                 face. Sire cumpainz, mar fut vostre

                 barnage...'

       1988   <u>A</u> <u>icest</u> <u>mort</u> <u>sur</u> <u>son</u> <u>cheval</u> <u>se</u> <u>pasment</u>.

1. 149 : 1989   As vus Rollant sur son cheval pasmet

                 <u>Et</u> <u>Oliver</u> <u>ki</u> <u>est</u> <u>a</u> <u>mort</u> <u>nafret</u>.

(2) <u>reprise</u> <u>bifurquée</u>: the repetition is from the middle, not
the end of the preceding laisse:

1. 267 : 3695   <u>Carles</u> <u>cevalchet</u> <u>e</u> <u>les</u> <u>vals</u> <u>a</u> <u>les</u> <u>munz</u>;

                 <u>Entresqu'a</u> <u>Ais</u> <u>ne</u> <u>volt</u> <u>prendre</u> <u>sujurn</u>.

                 Taut chevalchat qu'il descent al perrun.

                 <u>Cume</u> <u>il</u> <u>est</u> <u>en</u> <u>sun</u> <u>paleis</u> <u>halçur</u>,

                 Par ses messages mandet ses jugeors,

                 Baivers et Saisnes, Loherencs e Frisuns;

                 Alemans mandet, si mandet Bourguingnuns

                 E Peitevins et Normans et Bretuns,

                 De cels de France des plus saives que sunt.

                 Dès ore cumencet le plait de Gunelun.

1. 268 : 3705   <u>Li</u> <u>emperes</u> <u>est</u> <u>repairet</u> <u>d'Espaigne</u>

                 <u>E</u> <u>vient</u> <u>a</u> <u>Ais</u>, <u>al</u> <u>meillor</u> <u>sied</u> <u>de</u> <u>France</u>;

                 <u>Muntet</u> <u>el</u> <u>palais</u>, <u>est</u> <u>venut</u> <u>en</u> <u>la</u> <u>sale</u>.

                 As li Alde venue, une bele damisele.

                 Ço dist al rei: 'O est Rollant le catanie,

                 Ki me jurat cume sa per a prendre?'

                 Carles en ad e dulor e pesance,

                 Pluret des oilz, tiret sa barbe blance:

                 'Soer, cher' amie, d'hume mort me demandes.'

(3) A variant of (2), in which the corresponding lines are
    at the beginning of each laisse:

    1. 162 : 2184   Rolant s'en turnet, par le camp vait tut suls,

                         Cerclet les vals e si cercet les munz ...

                         Iloec truvat Gerin e Gerer sun cumpaigun,

                         E si truvat Berenger a Attun;

                         Iloec truvat Anseïs e Sansun,

                         Truvat Gerard le veill de Russillun.

    1. 163 : 2200   Rollant s'en turnet, le camp vait recercer,

                         Sun cumpaignun ad truvet, Oliver:

                         Encuntre sun piz estriet l'ad enbracet;

                         Si cum il poet a l'arcevesques en vent,

                         Sur un escut l'ad as altres culchet,

                         E l'arcevesque l'ad asols e seignet.

(4) Laisses parallèles, which describe actions of the same type
    but not identical; e.g., a series of boasts by different
    individuals:

    1. 72 : 894   Uns amurafles i ad de Balagues ...

          900   Devant Marsilie cil en est escriet:

                  'En Rencesvals irai mun cors juer!

                  Se truis Rollant, de mort serat finet

                  E Oliver e tux les .XII. pers.

    1. 73 : 909   Uns almaçurs i ad de Moraine ...

          911   Devant Marsilie ad faite sa vantance:

                  'En Rencesvals guierai me cumpaigne ...

          914   Se trois Rollant, de mort li duins fiance.

This particular series continues for several laisses.

(5) <u>Laisses</u> <u>similaires</u>, in which the same action is described
in two or three successive laisses but in a slightly different form:

1. 171 : 2297   Ço sent Rollant la veue ad perdue,

                    Met sei sur piez, quanqu'il poet s'esvertuet;

                    En sun visage sa culur ad perdue.

                    .X. colps i fiert par doel e par rancune.

1. 172 : 2312   Rollant ferit el perrun de sardonie

                    Cruist li acers, ne briest ne s'esprunie.

                    Quant il ço vit que n'en pout mie freindre,

                    A sei meïsme la cumencet a pleindre:

1. 173 : 2338   Rolland ferit en une perre bise.

                    Plus en abat que jo ne vos sai dire.

                    L'espee cruist, ne fruisset ne se brise,

                    Cuntre ciel amunt est resortie.

Professor Duggan, in his chapter "The Episode of Baligant," has calculated the number of laisses linked in each of
these five ways in the two major divisions of the poem
("Roland" and "Baligant"). Approximately 50% of the whole
poem consists of laisses linked in some way (54% of "Roland"
and 34% of "Baligant"), the most frequent type of linkage
being parallel (28% of "Roland" and 21% of "Baligant"). The
only major difference between the two parts is the "Baligant"
contains no <u>laisses</u> <u>similaires</u>, one of the most striking of
the Oxford poet's techniques which occurs at moments of in-
tense emotion in the poem, for example, the first horn scene
and that of Roland's death. This omission -- and the compara-

tive lack of elaboration and intensity of "Baligant," which
has led some critics to ignore it completely -- may be accounted
for by circumstances surrounding the actual transcription of
the Oxford version of the poem. The Venice IV manuscript
devotes considerable length to both the death of Aude and the
trial of Ganelon, which both receive relatively scant attention
in the Oxford version.

What is the function of these linked laisses in the poem
and how do they contribute to the development of the narrative?

It has already been pointed out that laisses similaires
occur at places of supreme interest and act as intensifiers of
emotion. The audience is compelled to regard the same events
more than once from a slightly different viewpoint (e.g.,
Roland and Durendal). The same is surely true of a repeated
motif, laisses parallèles, e.g., single combat in battle,
boasting before battle. These elaborations of a scene also
act to delay the forward movement of the plot but are not used
to heighten expectation -- this is something the poet is not
concerned with: we are told at the beginning that Ganelon is
the traitor and later that Charlemagne cannot return in time
to save Roland.

The importance of a particular motif or collection of
similar motifs, for the poet and his contemporary audience,
may be indicated therefore by the degree and complexity of
elaboration of the text. This interest may not be shared by
a modern reader who is considerably less concerned in a
practical way with deeds on horseback than was a twelfth

century audience. A parallel may be suggested with cinematic technique in which the climax of a fight is shown in extremely slow motion so that the audience can savor it to the full. I believe this device was first used by Akira Kurosawa, the Japanese director, in a scene from The Seven Samurai (1954) where Takashi Shimura kills the kidnapper of a child, and the dead man falls in slow motion. There are similar scenes in the same director's Yojimbo ("The Bodyguard") and in Arthur Penn's Bonny and Clyde (1967); the killing of Bonny and Clyde is shown in slow motion and repeated. In The Seven Samurai, Kurosawa also uses a great deal of repetition in the attacks by the bandits on the village that the samurai are defending and in the counter-attacks by the villagers and the samurai. The film has been criticized for this repetition and in the West only a heavily cut version is usually shown. But as Donald Richie says, "The complete three and one half hour film has an epic-like quality, due in part to the skillful repetition of events, which in the opinion of many puts it among the best films ever made not only in Japan but anywhere in the world."[4] In this quotation the word "epic," which is often misued in film criticism, has a valid meaning. In a traditional oral presentation, the singer of tales elaborates a particular scene if the audience's reaction is enthusiastic, in a manner similar to that of the Japanese film maker.

Just as the Acts, as subdivisions of the four themes, are arranged paratactically, framed and linked by a series of journeys, so are the laisses themselves put together para-

tactically. Each laisse is at once a separate unit, different
by way of its assonance from those which precede and follow
it, and also a member of a series in many cases linked by
repetition to one or more of its neighbors. The narrative,
on the level of the laisse, again proceeds by fits and starts,
now moving forward for a while, now marking time as a particular scene or motif is developed by the linking of laisses.

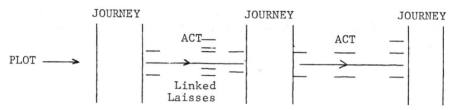

No distinction is made in this diagram regarding the kind of
linkage. The most delay in the forward motion of the action
(the most parataxis) is caused by multiple repitions as in a
series of parallel laisses, but the greatest intensity by the
similar laisses which the poet uses at the key points of his
narrative.

At the level of the individual laisse, many scholars
have commented on the paratactic structure of the Roland.
Auerbach gives examples of the parataxis in sentence-sequence,
and it can easily be shown that each line of each laisse is a
completed thought -- of the first one hundred and fifty verses,
in only five (vv. 17, 47, 48, 81, 83) is the thought not completed. Parry, Lord and others[5] have shown that this is also
true of the Greek oral epics and state that this "adding on
style" is a necessary characteristic of oral composition:
"absence of necessary enjambement is a characteristic of oral

composition and is one of the easiest touchstones to apply
in testing the orality of a poem."[6] I should like to suggest
that the paratactic structure of such a narrative also corresponds to the mode of thought of pre-literate people, who,
without the linear continuum of a written text, have not
learned first visually and then mentally to arrange their
mental processes in a logical linear continuum.[7]

In Chapter I, I referred to the work of H. and A.
Thornton (Time and Style) which characterizes the style of
early Greek authors as paratactic and what the Thorntons refer
to as "appositional ..., a plain, but emphatic statement of
the main item of the sentence or passage; expansions of their
initial statement ... and, frequently, a return to the initial
statement." As an example of this, I mentioned the first
chapter of Auerbach's Mimesis in which the recognition of
Odysseus by his old nurse Euryclea (Odyssey, Book 19) is
interrupted by seventy verses which relate the history of the
scar. Not until the story of the scar is finished with a
great deal of detail "does Euryclea, who recognized the scar
before the digression began, let Odysseus' foot fall back
into the basin." Auerbach goes on to point out that this is
by no means intended to increase tension in the reader --"the
element of suspense is very slight in the Homeric poems" --
but is part of "a uniformly illuminated, uniformly objective
present." This example, he says, "is not basically different
from the many passages in which a newly introduced character,
or even a newly appearing object or implement, though it be

in the thick of a battle, is described as to its nature and origin."[8]

These remarks of Auerbach's and the Thorntons' definition of appositional style describe perfectly many of the elements in the Roland. The example which immediately springs to mind is the entry of Baligant into the action of the poem. Like the discovery of Odysses' scar in the Odyssey, this is an element for which the author has not prepared us. After the motif which begins the third theme, we are abruptly informed that in the first year of Charlemagne's incursion into Spain Marsile had sent letters to Baligant requesting aid:

> 1. 189 - 2609   Li emperere par sa grant poestet
>
> .VII. anz tuz plens ad en Espaigne estet;
>
> Prent i chastels e alquantes citez.
>
> Li reis Marsilie s'en purcacet assez;
>
> Al premer an fist ses brefs seisler,
>
> En Babilonie Baligant ad mandet, ...

We are given the gist of Marsile's message, Baligant's delay and gathering of forces; his fleet is described, as are the embarkation of his troops, the voyage, the brilliant scene at night as they approach Spain, and so on. In fact, this "digression" continues until laisse 203 and includes the exchange of information between Baligant and Marsile, their meeting and surrender by Marsile of his lands to the Emir. This is a total of more than two hundred lines. Laisse 203 begins with a return to Charlemagne who awakes on the morning after his destruction of Marsile's army.

On a smaller scale, the introduction of a new character -- particularly one in a series such as in a succesion of parallel laisses -- is often treated in a similar way: the name is given, the character's place of origin, relationship to other characters, physical description; his attitude toward the enemy, a speech by him or his actions in battle may be included. The laisse ends and we frequently hear no more of him. As has already been pointed out, this kind of repetition serves to concentrate the attention of the listener and to give him the pleasure of appreciating an embellishment of the narrative movement but does not serve to advance the movement. This is not to say, of course, that there is not flexibility of poetic art within the motif-formula system, as J. J. Duggan has shown. With these linked laisses one has the impression of repeated units, of a recurring cycle of action, and this is the point which the Thorntons in their study are concerned with: they suggest a connection between the cyclical style of the narratives they consider and a cyclic attitude toward time in the societies whose cultural products they discuss. But they do not demonstrate in any great detail the patterns of time included in the narratives in which they are interested. This, however, is something that I should like to do.

What references to time are there in the _Roland_, and how are they related to one another? Are they connected in any way to the narrative patterns we have already pointed out?

There are a few points in the poem when saints' days are referred to: the feast of St. Michael is mentioned three times, twice by Blancandrin in Marsile's council scene (lines 37 and 53) and then again as the message is delivered to Charlemagne (line 152). All of these concern the date by which Marsile will arrive at Aix to receive baptism into the Christian Church. The date of this feast was then September 29th. Ganelon's trial takes place on the feast of St. Silvester (line 3746) which is December 31st.

Periods of time mentioned include "dous cenz anz" or ".II.C. anz" (524; 539; 552), the age of Charlemagne; "cent anz" (664), the period for which Galne was deserted; "set (or ".VII.") anz" (2; 197; 266; 2610; 2736), the duration of Charlemagne's stay in Spain. "An" (653; 972; 2613) refers first to Marsile's promise to send Ganelon presents every year ("ja mais n'iert an"), second to Margariz' boast to have conquered France within a year ("jus qu'a un an"), and third to Marsile's dispatch of letters to Baligant in the first year of Charlemagne's invasion of Spain ("al premer an").

"Meis" is also used three times: first, Marsile gives Blancandrin the message for Charlemagne that he will join the emperor and become Christian ("ja einz ne verrat passer cest premer meis" [83]); second, Ganelon repeats this message after his return to Charlemagne ('ja ne verrez cest premer meis passet" [693]); and third, Marsile gives Baligant's messengers advice for the Emir regarding Charlemagne ("cunquis l'avrat d'oi cest jur en un meis" [2751]).

In none of these examples do either 'year' or 'month' have any function in the narrative patterning of the poem

itself -- they either refer to events outside the action or
to events which do not take place or are incomplete.

The terms which are used, however, are those which
refer to the cycle of light and dark: "albe" (three times);
"matin (six); "jor," "jur," etc. (thirty-seven); "vespere"
(six); " noit," "nuit" (sixteen). As has been shown in
Chapter II, there is no connected linear sequence of time
units in the Roland, so these time references must function
in some other way. Let us see if we can discover any regular
patterning in their occurrence.

Of the thirty-seven occurrences of the word for 'day'
("jor," "jurz," "jur," "jurn"), almost half have nothing to
do with the efflux of time during the action of the poem;
most of these are related to emotion rather than to time and
are usually used in sequences of linked laisses (one of the
functions of which we have shown to be to increase the emotional enjoyment of the audience). For example, the sequence
of boasts by the pagan Saracen warriors before the battle
(laisses 71ff) includes:

971 'jamais n'ert jurn qu'il n'en ait doet e ire'

915 'jamais n'ert jor que Carles ne se pleignet'

This is preceded by ominous narrative comments about the evil
of the time to come:

813 une bataille lur livrat le jur pesme

816 le jur passerent Franceis a grant dulur

1406 Malvais servis le jur li rendit Guenes

The prophetic boasts of the Saracens are fulfilled in the

plaint (planctus) of Charlemagne when he reaches the battlefield:

> 2901   jamais n'ert jurn de tei n'aie dulur
>
> 2915   jamais n'ert jur que ne plur ne n'en plaigne
>
> 2927   quant cil est morz ki tuz jurz nos cadelet

Ganelon twice includes 'day' in his criticisms of Roland:

> 390   'kar chascun jur de mort s'abandunet'
>
> 1780   'pur un sul levre vait tute jur cornant'

In neither of these cases is "jur" used to indicate the passage of time. "Turz jurz" (1882) and "cascun jur" (2502)
are each used again, once by Turpin to describe the behavior
of monks, and once by the narrator referring to the color
changes of the sword Joyeuse. The connotations are of affective or generalized behavior rather than time either as
duration or sequence. Similarly, the fifteen occurrences of
the word for 'today' ("hoi" or "oi") refer almost exclusively
to negative qualities; for example, separation, death, curses,
or weeping. In no case is 'today' contrasted temporally with
other days, nor does it ever occur in narrative but only in
direct speech. It is connected, therefore, to the speaker's
feelings. In no occurrence of any of these words is there
any indication of duration. No day is described as long or
short, no action is said to last the whole or part of a day.
Time, as we said in Chapter I, has two elements -- sequence
and duration. The Roland, as we shall see, embodies the
element of sequence, but that of duration is absent.

The remaining occurrences of 'day', and those of 'night',

'evening', 'morning' and 'dawn', fall into two categories,
that of description (which also precedes action) and that
which clearly marks the beginning or ending of a block of
action. The descriptive category usually includes the verb
'to be' while the marking category includes a verb denoting
ending, beginning, or change from one state to another; e.g.,
"passet la noit, si apert le cler jor" (line 3675). But it
is important to note that in neither type of phrase is action
consequent upon the time indication -- there is no causal or
grammatical connection. We have 'Dawn broke. The king heard
Mass.' We do not have 'After sunrise, the king heard Mass'
nor 'Night fell and then Charlemagne slept.' In other words,
the relation between the celestial event and the action which
follows is paratactic in every case.

First we shall consider the descriptive category and
then see if the marking category is arranged in any kind of
pattern related to the narrative structure we have previously
set out.

The first example of description occurs after Blancandrin
has arrived at Charlemagne's camp and delivered Marsile's
message: "Bels fut li vespres e li soleilz fut cler" (157).
There is an indication of time of day ("vespres"), though no
sense of change. Appropriately, the lodging of the visitors
follows -- there is a double function, description and initia-
tion.

With the arming scene of the Saracens, however, there
is no sense of the time of day, but the phrase here does

precede action:

> 1002 Clers fut li jurz e bels fut li soleilz:
>
> N'unt guarnement que fut ne reflambeit
>
> Sunent mil grailles por ço que plus bel seit:
>
> Granz est la noise, si l'orïent Franceis.

Similarly:

> 2512 Clere est la noit e la lune luisant.
>
> Carles se gist, mais doel ad de Rollant
>
> E d'Oliver le peseit mult forment ...

In the next laisse, Charlemagne begins to dream.

The description of Baligant's fleet arriving at night includes:

> 2635 Par la noit la mer en est plus bele

and the disembarkation is preceded by:

> 2646 Clers est li jurz e li soleilz luisant.

The final example of this type is again part of the description of an army before battle:

> 3345 Clers fut le jurz e li soleilz luisanz.
>
> Les oz sont beles e les cumpaignes granz.

In each case, the verb concerned is not of change --
we are shown an indefinite part of the day or night, always
with adjectives of beauty and brightness: "bels," "clers,"
"luisanz," whether day or night is being referred to. This
is an indication of the non-objective attitude toward time
-- the day does not exist as a simple quantitative unit, but
has qualities of light, emotional overtones, or is closely
linked to action.

Now we shall look at the expressions which mark changes
in the daily cycle, and which are connected more clearly to
turning points in the action of the narrative. Not surprisingly,
the most frequent indication is to 'dawn', with seven references, though at least two obviously refer to the same day.
These references mark the end or the beginning of significant
action:

A 162   La noit demurent tresque vint al jur cler.

         Li empereres est par matin levet ...

         Ses baruns mandet pur sun cunseill finer:

B 667   Par main en l'albe, si cum li jurz esclairet,

         Guenes li quens est venuz as herberges.

         Li empereres est par matin levet; ...

671   Sur l'erbe verte estut devant sun tref.

C 737   Tresvait la noit e apert la clere albe.

         Par me cel host.

         Li empereres mult fierement chevalchet.

The designation of Roland to the rearguard by Ganelon immediately
follows.

D 2568   Li angles Deu ço ad mustret al barun.

         Carles se dort tresqu'al demain, al cler jur.

This follows the two dreams Charlemagne has after his destruction
of Marsile's army; and the dreams foretell the advent of
Baligant.

E 2845   Al matin, quant primes pert li albe,

         Esveillez est li emperere Carles.

This is one of the very few examples of a logical or grammatical connection between a time-phrase and the action which
follows it. The couplet is important since it begins the
laisse which returns us to Charlemagne after the "digression"
of Baligant's preparation and arrival which we discussed
above as an example of the appositional style. Since this
dawn is followed at once by Charlemagne's return to Roncevaux,
we must assume it is the same dawn as in D above, in which
the emperor dreams of Baligant's arrival following the defeat
of Marsile. There is no reason to imagine that the emperor
would waste any time in returning to the scene of his nephew's
death.

F 3675   Passet la noit, si apert le cler jor.

De Sarraguce Carles guarnist les turs;
Saragossa has be captured. Charlemagne takes with him Brami-
mode and begins his journey back to France, leaving a gar-
rison in the city.

G 3731   La noit la guaitent entresqu'a l'ajurnee.

Lunc un alter belement l'enterrerent.
After the death of Aude, the nuns keep vigil until dawn, then
they bury her. This marks the end of the (brief) partici-
pation of Aude in the action.

The word for 'night' obviously frequently goes with 'day'
in phrases which we have already considered describing the
change from the one to the other, but there are also a few
cases in which night_fall_ is marked:

A 717   Tresvait le jur, la noit est aserie.

Carles se dort, li empereres riches.

Charlemagne's first set of dreams follows, foretelling the
treachery of Ganelon and a battle.

B   3658   Passet li jurz, la noit est aserie;

Clere est las lune e les esteiles flambient.

This is the only place in the poem where important action
takes place at night, though of course the moon is bright.
The narrative describes here the destruction of "les sinagoges
e les mahumeries," the smashing of "les ymagenes e trestutes
les ydeles," and the hanging, burning, or (otherwise) killing
of unrepentant infidels. Perhaps this destruction of pos-
sessions and people of darkness is appropriately placed in
the night-time hours.

C   3991   Passett li jurz, la nuit est aserie.

Culchez s'est le reis en sa cambre voltice.

Charlemagne has carried out the punishment of Ganelon and
baptized Bramimonde. This couplet precedes his dream in
which he is told to gather his forces, since the Saxons are
in revolt. This ending is clearly the overture of the next
beginning -- the Charlemagne cycle never ends.

There is one example of the change from day to evening:

3560   Passet li jurz, si turnet a la vespree.

Franc e paien i fierent des espees.

This is not a point of change but a gradual change as "turnet"
implies. The action of the battle begins earlier and continues
after, but this couplet is followed by the single combat
between Charlemagne and Baligant -- obviously a turning-point.

In most of the cases of "marking-function," the expression occurs at the beginning or ending of the laisse (nine of the twelve examples just given). As with the narrative elements, there is a connection between laisses and other breaks in the poem's sequence.

I believe I have shown in the preceding few pages that the words and phrases connected with daytime are used in three different ways: first to emphasize the emotional content of a scene, secondly to describe the brilliance, in terms of light, of a scene, and thirdly to function as markers of beginning or ending of a sequence of action (functions two and three may be combined). In none of these is contained any feeling of objective linear time -- there is always a qualitative connotation, whether of emotion, beauty, or a link with action. The word "tens" itself is similarly qualitative and in three cases it refers to human life directly: "si ad sun tens uset" (523); "tut i laisset sun tens" (1419); "de sun tens n'i ad mais" (3840). Once it means 'always': "tuz tens m'avez servit" (1858); and once 'it's time' to do something: "tens est del herberger" (2482).

The same points of the daily cycle are used again and again, however, and I should now like to see if there is any regularity in their appearance and if in any way their occurrence matches the structural divisions we discovered earlier. Here is the sequence:

ACT	LAISSE	vv			BLANCANDRIN'S JOURNEY
I	11	157	vespres	Evening	Blancandrin's embassy

ACT	LAISSE	vv			Rest
		162	noit	Night	Charlemagne's council
II		162	al jur cler	Dawn	
III		163	matin		
					GANELON'S JOURNEY AND RETURN
	53	667	albe	Dawn	
IV	54	669	matin		
		END OF THEME I			CHARLEMAGNE TO RONCEVAUX
I	56	717	noit	Nightfall	Ominous dreams
	58	737	albe	Dawn	Designation of rear-guard
					FRANKS LEAVE
II	79	1002	jurz	Day (unspecific)	Battle
					CHARLEMAGNE'S RETURN
	137	1807	vespres	Evening	Marsile's forces destroyed
III					CHARLEMAGNE'S PURSUIT
	184	2512	noit	Night	Ominous dreams
IV	186	2569	al cler jur	Dawn	
		END OF THEME II			
I	190	2635	noit	Night	BALIGANT'S VOYAGE
	191	2644	noit	Night	Baligant's arrival
II	192	2646	jurz	Day (unspecific)	Baligant's disembarkation
III, IV					BALIGANT'S MESSENGERS TO MARSILE AND RETURN
V	203	2845	albe	Dawn	(same as 2569)

ACT	LAISSE	vv			
VI					CHARLEMAGNE TO RONCEVAUX
	240	3345	jurz	Day	Preparations for battle
VII	258	3560	vespree	Evening	Battle; Charlemagne's pursuit
VIII	266	3658	noit	Nightfall	Capture of Saragossa
	267	3675	jor	Dawn	Garrison set
			END OF THEME III		CHARLEMAGNE TO AIX
I	269	3731	noit...a l'ajurnee	Night:Dawn	Death of Aude
					VASSALS TO AIX
II	291	3991	noit	Nightfall	Ganelon's trial; ominous dreams
					CHARLEMAGNE TO SAXONY

There is some agreement between the narrative pattern
and the temporal pattern -- each of the first three themes
ends with a dawn scene, and the fourth ends with Charlemagne
asleep, presumably about to set off on another journey after
another council scene at dawn to combat the Saxons. For the
most part, the journeys and the Acts which we outlined earlier
match the pattern of times of day, but what is immediately
obvious is that the sequence of the times of day is perfectly
regular with one exception. The sequence is Evening - Night -
Dawn to begin with, and one would expect Evening or Night to
follow, but they do not. The situation is the journey of
Ganelon to Marsile and the treacherous agreement. Other
council scenes are preceded with a time-phrase, and other

standard elements are present in this once (laisse 31) -- the
throne, covered in costly material, under the pine tree, the
assembly of warriors, and so on. But there is no time-reference
either to the arrival of Blancandrin and Ganelon nor to Marsile's arising. Here, perhaps, Turold or the scribe nodded,
and omitted one of the usual formulas.

With this exception, the sequence continues regularly
and cyclically; NIGHTFALL - DAWN - (mid?) DAY - EVENING -
NIGHT - DAWN to the end of theme II. Theme III begins with
a flashback, as we have shown, so that the NIGHT - DAWN at
the end of Theme II is the same as the NIGHT - DAWN at the
beginning of Theme II, but in any case the sequence is not
irregular. Theme III continues: DAY - EVEING - NIGHTFALL -
DAWN, where it ends. Theme IV contains NIGHT till DAWN, then
NIGHT, in which we leave Charlemagne sleeping. We must point
out, of course, that these are not successive days -- each
element, separated by a journey or not, may be a considerable
objective duration from its predecessor and successor. But
the poet, true, I suggest, to his inborn notion of repetitive
cyclic patterning of both time and events, automatically re-
produces the natural day cycle in his poem. In fact, the
consistency of the temporal cycle DAWN - EVENING - NIGHT is
greater than that of the narrative cycle of Themes divided
by journeys with Acts. Both, however, are patterns of the
same type -- repetitive, paratactic/appositional, cyclic.
The narrative and the time-structure which informs it proceed
like a hoop rolled by a child along a sidewalk.

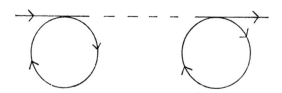

The motion of the whole is forward, but any point on the cir-
cumference of the hoop moves in a circle.

The structure and unity of <u>Beowulf</u> have been critical
problems for a long time; many editors and scholars, such as
Klaeber, refer to its "lack of steady advance," its lack of
"lucidity, proportion, and finish of form as required by
modern texts" (lviii and lxviii), to the loose manner in
which the two main parts of the poem are held together (li),
and to "the facts of Geatish history [which] are a little too
in evidence and retard the narrative of the second part rather
seriously" (liv). But at least since the publication of
J. R. R. Tolkein's article in 1936,[9] scholars have taken a
closer look at the way the poem is put together, and the manner
in which the so-called digressions and episodes illuminate
the character of the hero and add background to the action.

Several of these scholars,[10] including Klaeber, refer
to the non-linear style of the poem: Nist calls it "cyclic"
and "contrapuntal" (p. 312-13); Leyerle calls the structure
"interlace" (p. 1); Blomfield says that "tales and allusions
... are grouped in a wide sweep around the hero's character
... the structure is not sequential but complemental" (pp. 57,
60); Bonjour mentions the ease with which the poet "created

a number of various links between the different episodes and some aspect of the main story" (p. 71), while Bartlett characterizes Beowulf "as a tapestry, which presents its pictures in a series of panels" (p. 7). There seems to be, then, general agreement that Beowulf is not constructed in a linear manner.

Professor Tolkien talks of a balance between two main divisions of the poem which is analogous to the balance between the two alliterating half-lines of which the poem is composed, while others suggest that the poem falls rather neatly into three sections -- or three sittings for oral presentation (Sisam, p. 4; Nist, p. 312). This disagreement can be resolved by a realization that Tolkien's divisions are based on time -- fifty years separate the actions of Beowulf as a young hero and as an aged king, while Sisam is considering oral presentation of three performances and also action -- the hero's three fights.

There are no stanzas to compare with the laisses of the Roland, and the smallest unit of structure is the half-line, connected to its second half by alliteration. Unlike Roland, Beowulf contains many run-on lines which the poet "uses ... with remarkable ease and flexibility" (Brodeur, p. 2).

An important characteristic of the poem's style is that of repetition and accumulation, and of repetition with variation. This is true on the level of single words and of groups of descriptive phrases (Brodeur, pp. 39ff; Blomfield,

p. 60). It has been pointed out that the technique of variation is used "to communicate emotion with intensity and depth [although] by its very nature [it] slows down the pace of the narrative" (Brodeur, p. 51). Variation is "very rare in lines which report the action and heavier in those that communicate the feelings of the participants" (Brodeur, p. 56). Bonjour, in an article on anticipation, [11] points out the way in which the poet's use of this concept heightens the emotional content of the poem and Brodeur comments on the way in which "allusions to heroic legend act as anrichment and adornment" (p. 133).

These general remarks suggest a similarity to the Roland in the way that two basic elements in the narrative function: there are those which concern the sequence of action itself, and there are those which elaborate or ornament the narrative, retarding its movement but increasing emotional content or adding depth.

There are, however, some major differences between the Roland and Beowulf: in the Roland the elaborations occur within the general time-framework of the poem, are directly connected to the action (for example, a series of laisses describing a succession of similar actions such as boasting), but in Beowulf the "digressions" frequently refer to events outside the time-system of the poem -- to mythic happenings such as the Creation (lines 90b-98), the punishment of Cain (lines 107b-114), or to historical events which are in the past with respect to the audience and narrator of the poem, but in the future of the characters <u>within</u> the poem (for example, Hygelac's death in Friesland, lines 2354[b]-2396). We should remember also that the dragon fight takes place fifty years after Beowulf's defeat of Grendel and Grendel's mother.

Another difference between <u>Beowulf</u> and the <u>Roland</u> concerns the journeys. We showed that in the <u>Roland</u> the journeys made convenient divisions or frames between blocks of action and were outside time -- the armies appear to be transported almost instantaneously from one place to another -- but in <u>Beowulf</u> this is not the case. Journeys -- of which there are many, though most not covering a great distance -- frequently contain significant action or description even though their duration is not often referred to. For example, Alain Renoir[12] has brilliantly illuminated Grendel's night-time journey down to Heorot on the night when Beowulf is keeping guard, showing in cinematic terms how the monster occupies a greater and greater proportion of the audience's visual field as he approaches Heorot. The triumphant journey of the warriors from the mere after tracking the injured Grendel there includes a <u>scop</u> composing verses on Beowulf's victory as well as horse races on the way home (lines 868-918), and the pursuit of Grendel's mother contains a description of the country through which the Danes travelled (lines 1400-1415).

Let us now divide <u>Beowulf</u> into its three thematic divisions and see what we can make of the narrative patterns, using Sisam's three-part scheme[13]: the fight against Grendel (lines 1-1250);

the encounter with Grendel's mother (1251-2199); the fight against the dragon (2200-3182).

I: THE FIGHT AGAINST GRENDEL

Line	Scene	NARRATIVE	Line	Scene	ELABORATION
58 - 82^a	1	Genealogy of Hrothgar and the building of Heorot	1 - 52	A	Origin of Scylding line; Scyld's burial
86 - 90^a	2	Introduction of Grendel	82^b - 85	B	Fate of Heorot
99 - 107^a	3	Grendel's malice	90^b - 98	C	Song of Creation
115 - 418	4	Grendel's raids (for twelve years); despair of Hrothgar; councils; idol worship; news reaches Beowulf; preparation for journey; coast-guard's challenge; arrival at Heorot; welcome	107^b - 114	D	Cain's punishment and his offspring
424^b - 459	5	Beowulf expresses purpose; his power and determination	419 - 424^a	E	Youthful adventures of Beowulf
473 - 498	6	Hrothgar recounts Grendel's deeds; joy in feast	459 - 472	F	Settling of Ecgtheow's feud begun by Beowulf's father
			499 - 589	G	Unferth 'intermezzo'; swimming contest with Breca

Line	Scene	NARRATIVE	Line	Scene	ELABORATION
590 - 874^a	7	Beowulf criticizes Unferth; Beowulf's determination; Wealtheor serves wine; end of feast; Hrothgar leaves; Beowulf's boast; Grendel's attack; the battle; Grendel flees; journey to the mere and return; scop composes poem on Beowulf	874^b- 915	H	Stories of Sigemund and Heremod
916 - 1068	8	Horse racing; Hrothgar's thanks to God and praise of Beowulf; decoration of Heorot; rewards; minstrel at feast	1069 -1159^a	I	The Finnsburg tale
1159^b- 1196	9	Wealtheow's speech; gives necklace to Beowulf	1197 -1201	J	Allusions to Eormenric and Hama -- the necklace
1215 - 1250	10	Wealtheow's speech; feast; Hrothgar retires; sleep	1202 -1214	K	The fall of Hygelac

II: ENCOUNTER WITH GRENDEL'S MOTHER

Line	Scene	NARRATIVE	Line	Scene	ELABORATION
1251 - 1689ᵃ	1	Attack by Grendel's mother; pursuit to the mere; underwater battle; victory for Beowulf; return to Heorot	1689ᵇ- 1693	A	Beowulf's destruction of the gigantas
1694 - 1709ᵃ	2	Hrothgar's praise of Beowulf	1709ᵇ- 1722ᵃ	B	Decline and fall of Here-mod
1722ᵇ- 1724ᵃ	3	Hrothgar's advice to Beowulf	1724ᵇ- 1757	C	Sermon against pride and avarice
1758 - 1931ᵃ	4	Hrothgar's advice to Beowulf; sleep; rewards; farewells; journey to Sweden; arrival	1931ᵇ- 1962	D	Story of Thryth, wife of Offa
1963 - 2031	5	to Hygelac's hall; Beowulf's welcome; Beowulf's speech begins	2032 - 2066	E	Feud between Danes and Heathobards
2067 - 2183ᵃ	6	Beowulf's report; Beowulf's gifts to Hygelac	2183ᵇ- 2189	F	Beowulf's inglorious youth
2190 - 2199	7	Hygelac's gifts to Beowulf			

III: FIGHT WITH THE DRAGON

Line	Scene	NARRATIVE	Line	Scene	ELABORATION
2200 - 2231^a	1	Beowulf's fifty years rule; dragon's ravages; treasure disturbed	2231^b- 2278	A	Origin of treasure; survivor's lament
2278 - 2354^a	2	Dragon's 300 year vigil; dragon's ravages; news gets to Beowulf; hero's preparations	2354^b- 2396	B	Geatish history; Hygelac's death; Beowulf's swimming exploit; his guardianship of Heardred; second series of Swedish wars
2397 - 2424	3	Journey to dragon's cave	2425 - 2508^a	C	Beowulf tells Geatish history; King Hrethel; the death of Herebald [2444-2462^a: lament of the father]; earlier war with Swedes; Beowulf's slaying of Dæghrefn
2510 - 2625^b	4	Beowulf's vow; battle with dragon	2611 - 2625^a	D	Weohstan's slaying of Eanmund in later Swedish war; history of weapon
2625^b- 2910	5	Death of dragon; Beowulf gives thanks to God, dies; cowards' return to Wiglaf's criticism; news spreads			

Line	Scene	NARRATIVE	Line	Scene	ELABORATION
			2910[b]- 3007[a]	E	Geatish history; Hygelac's fall; battle at Ravenswood in the earlier Swedish war
3007[b]- 3050	6	Preparation for funeral	3051 - 3068	F	Curse on treasure
3076 - 3182	7	Wiglaf's speech; funeral pyre prepared; final ceremonies			

I: THE FIGHT AGAINST GRENDEL

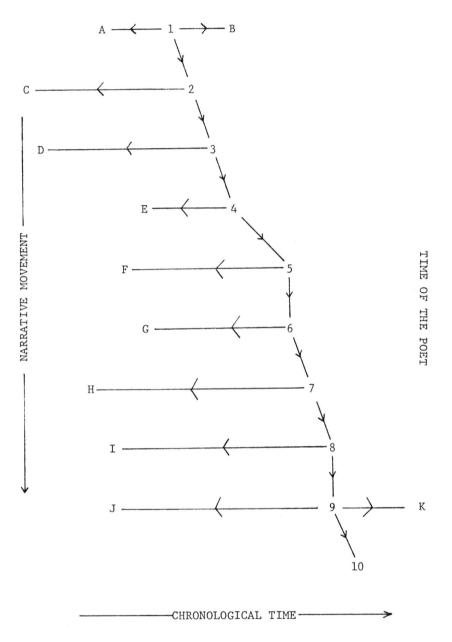

II: ENCOUNTER WITH GRENDEL's MOTHER

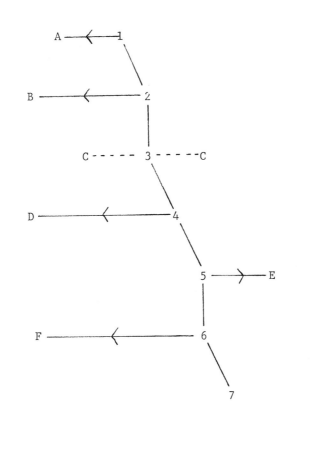

III: FIGHT WITH THE DRAGON

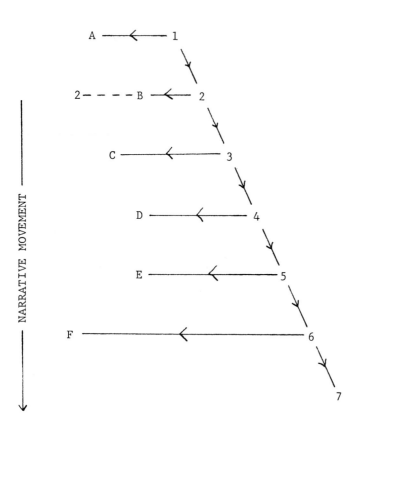

From these necessarily simplified diagrams one can
quickly see the relationships between the narrative flow and
the elaborating elements which retard that flow but which
clearly add historical and psychological depths to the events
and to the characters of the poem. In the Roland, we saw how
the repetitions of the linked laisses describing similar
events increased the intensity of emotion conveyed in scenes
of particular interest. In Beowulf, however, the elaborating
elements act as intensifiers in a completely different way.
Present joy is contrasted with future unhappiness, successful
life is contrasted with inevitable death, glorious beauty with
ultimate destruction: "It is always when something looks or
is described as splendid, stable, or peaceful, or when friendly
people are in the midst of rejoicings, that [these anticipa-
tions] take place" (Bonjour, p. 299). It is not only antici-
pations that function in this way, however -- in fact, more
often the elaboration compares present triumph with past
disasters, or present success with past failure.

But the point I wish to make is that without exception
the elaborations are placed in a different time-setting from
the main narrative: usually this is the past but occasionally
it is the future. Again and again the present is contrasted
with the past. The diagrams show that almost every narrative
"scene" is modified or qualified by an appropriate elaborating
element. Whereas in the Roland blocks of narrative were
framed by journeys which were without time and contained no
action, in Beowulf each block of narrative is separated from

the next by a journey (usually backwards) in time. The
narrative structures of the two poems can be seen then as
similar in that they are non-linear, but in the Roland
elaboration takes place within the action-black framed by the
journeys -- time stops; in Beowulf, however, the elaboration
is part of the frame and there is a jump in time, usually
backwards, but sometimes forwards. In the Roland the journeys
involve jumps in space; in Beowulf the frames concern jumps
in time.

It is true that the past is not totally ignored in the
Roland; when Charlemagne hears Roland's horn, Ganelon says
that Roland is willing to spend a whole day pursuing one hare
(laisse 134), and he tells Blancandrin that Roland rode on a
frivolous journey to fetch Charlemagne a scarlet apple (laisse
29). There are also references to Marsile's previous perfidy
in killing Basin and Basile -- but all these events are connected to the personal history of one or another of the characters in the poem, they are all part of the group experience.
In Beowulf, as was demonstrated in Chapter II, from the beginning we can distinguish three forms of the past. There are
mythic or sacred events such as the Creation and the history
of Cain's offspring, there are historical or quasi-historical
events involving the genealogy of Hrothgar, the stories of
Heremod and Ecgtheow, and there are events within the personal
experience of the characters of the poem. The latter includes,
of course, Beowulf's inglorious youth and his youthful
achievements. From part three of the poem we get another

perspective of the past. Fifty years have elapsed since
Beowulf's return to Sweden and we hear of happenings which
took place between the hero's return and the beginning of
the dragon's ravages, that is, during the time outside the
actual narrative but within the time-frame of the whole poem.
What was in the future for part two is now the past; this
includes most of the Geatish history -- the fall of Hygelac,
Beowulf's exploits and the Swedish wars. For the poet and
his audience, of course, everything which occurs in the poem
is in the past. But the expanse of fifty years between Beowulf's triumphant return to Sweden and the beginning of the
dragon conflict is filled with events -- it is given existence
by the recitation of events occurring within it. The frame
of the narrative scenes is itself highly decorated.

In the diagrams of chronological time and narrative
movement, I have tried to show, roughly, the relative chronology of the elaborating elements. One can quickly see that
there is no obvious pattern in the arrangement of these
elements -- one might expect that the early part of the narrative would refer to events more distant in time than would
later parts of the narrative, but this is not so. The reason
for the selection of particular stories is related to their
function as elaborating a particular part of the narrative.
Even in part three, which contains a preponderance of history,
one hears about the second series of Swedish wars (in 2354^{b}-
2396) before the earlier (2425-2508^{a}), there are then references to the later wars (2611-2625^{a}) followed by another

mention of the fall of Hygelac and the earlier wars again
(2910^b-3007^a). Events of the historical part do not seem to
be distinguished from one another -- they are all (almost
equally) "past." But they are clearly distinguished from
mythic events (the Creation) and events of personal experience
(Beowulf's youthful deeds). There are important differences,
then, regarding the past from the ideas embodied in the
Roland to those of Beowulf: the latter represent concepts
much closer to a linear concept of time in which past, present,
and future are clearly distinguished.

We have seen how the narrative patterns of Beowulf are
similar to those of the Roland in that the narrative flow of
each is interrupted by elaborations which make a linear
structure impossible to discern. But while the elaborations
of the Roland are placed within the same time-frame of the
poem, those of Beowulf are explicitly outside -- they are set
in a contrasted past or future. Edward B. Irving, Jr.[14] has
shown how "oð" and "oððæt" ('until') are used to link scenes
which contrast success or the hope of success to failure or
disaster. "There are thirty-six instances of these words
in Beowulf .... Thirteen [are] 'neutral', that is, carry no
specific emotional charge" (p. 31). Irving demonstrates that
of the remaining twenty-three occurrences "bad" follows "good,"
and "bad" follows "bad" in thirteen. This confirms the pattern of contrasts I have just pointed out between "narrative"
and "elaboration" -- there is a temporal relation in these
juxtapositions indicated by 'until' -- but in no example

which Irving mentions does 'until' link "narrative" to "elaboration." The pattern of 'until' occurs <u>within</u> either narrative or elaboration, so that Irving's pattern confirms the
pattern I describe but is structurally inside it -- wheels
within wheels, as it were. The use of 'until' in <u>Beowulf</u>
produces a kind of temporal relation between events which is
totally lacking in the <u>Roland</u>.

In the <u>Roland</u> we saw how the action of the poem is
related to the natural time-cycle of day and night, with
important events linked closely to particular parts of this
cycle. Except for the destruction of Saragossa with the
slaughter of its pagan inhabitants, all action occurs in
daylight, frequently beginning with day and ending in the
evening. Let us examine <u>Beowulf</u> and see what reference to
time the poem contains and if the patterns of time can be
related to the patterns of events.

The first and most obvious difference regarding the
day/night cycle is that much of the action of <u>Beowulf</u> takes
place at night -- in fact the contrast between light and
dark, good and evil is an important feature of the poem.[15]
Grendel, his mother, and the dragon are all creatures of the
dark who actively dislike daylight and everything connected
with it. This contrast will certainly affect the times of
day at which action begins and concludes.

In <u>Beowulf</u> there are no references to fixed dates such
as the couple of feast-days mentioned in the <u>Roland</u>. Periods
of time longer than a day are based on three different words:

"gēar," "missēre," and "winter." "Gēar" and its compound "gēardagum" occur five times, but in no case does it mean anything as precise as a year. In line 1134, "gēar" means 'spring'; in lines 1, 1354, and 2233, "gēardagum" means 'long ago'; and "geara," in 2664, similarly means 'long since'. "Missēre" (four occurrences) means 'season' in the sense of 'half-year' and is used in the computation of time. "Fela missēra" (153; 2620) implies an imprecise though long period of time, 'many years'; "hund missēra" (1498; 1769) could be translated as 'fifty years' but again may be taken as equivalent to 'a long time' (compare the Biblical forty years in the wilderness; forty days and forty nights). "Winter" and its compounds occur much more often (fifteen times) and are used essentially in two ways; first, as referring to the winter season, the cold weather (516; 1128; 1132; 1136), the last three of which refer to the same winter. Secondly, to mean 'year', in the computation of time; the range is from a thousand years to seven: "þusend wintra" (3050); "þrēo hund wintra" (2278); "fīftig wintra" (2209; 2733); "twelf wintra" (147); "syfan wintre" (2428); "wintra worn" (264); "wintra lyt" (1927). There is also the connection of many years of age with wisdom in the combination "wintrum frōd" (1724; 2114; 2277). There are no references to 'weeks' or 'months'. There is similarity to the use of comparable terms in the Roland: the "þusend wintra" and "þrēo hund wintra" refer to the corroded appearance of the dragon-hoard and the period the dragon has been guarding the treasure respectively. I

think we may take these as equivalent to the great age of
Charlemagne and Baligant, and the period for which Galne was
deserted. The "fīftig wintra" and "hund missēra" are periods
of rule of different characters -- Beowulf, Hrothgar, and
Grendel's mother. Again, it seems that thse may be taken to
be paradigmatic rather than syntagmatic. "Twelf wintra" and
"syfan wintre" refer to the duration of Grendel's ravages
and the age at which Beowulf says he was fostered by Hrethel;
neither of these functions within the narrative itself.

We come, then, as in the Roland to the functional cycle
of day and night. The occurrences of the words for 'day',
'night', 'morning' and 'evening' are remarkably close in
number to those of the Roland with an obvious exception, that
is, "niht." There is an important difference in emphasis,
however; in the Roland, "jor" in the singular refers exclusively to 'daylight', while in Beowulf, although this is
common, there is also the more general meaning of duration,
especially in plural compounds such as "līfdagas," "lǣndagas."
In the Roland there are none of these compounds and only one
plural (851, III, "jurz"). "Dæg" and its compounds, thirty-
nine; "morgen," etc., nine; "ǣfen," etc., seven; "niht," etc.,
twenty-nine. The frequency of "niht" is almost twice that of
"nuit" in the Roland, which is not surprising.

As with the Roland, in Beowulf almost half of the occurrences of the word for 'day' are connected to emotion rather
than the passage of time. Without exception the emotion is
a negative one, since the association is with death directly

or by implication. There is also an interesting symmetry in the use of these phrases, an almost perfect balance between the two main parts of the poem which bears out Tolkien's description of the poem as "essentially a balance, an opposition of ends and beginnings ... [an] intensely moving contrast between youth and age"(p.34).

The seventeen references to the day of death are divided between the first and second parts of the poem, that is, between lines 1-2200 and 2201-3182. There are nine in the first part and eight in the second. If we exclude the single reference of this kind to Grendel's mother (1622, "oflēt līfdagas"), there is a perfect symmetry between Beowulf's battles with Grendel and with the dragon. In each part, the first and last reference is generalized or unrelated directly to the narrative, while those in between connect (with one exception) to the deaths of Grendel and Beowulf respectively.

PART ONE

186b-187a   Wēl bi ð þǣm þe mōt / æfter dēaðdæge

Although this refers to the joy of the Christian who is accepted by God after death, the setting is the heathen acts of Hrothgar's men in vain attempts to excorcise Grendel.

636b-638   'Ic gefremman sceal / eorlīc ellen, oþ ðe endedæg on þisse meodurealle mīnne gebīdden!'

Here Beowulf is boasting that he will either conquer Grendel or die.

718   Nǣfre hē on aldordagum   ǣr nē siþðan

756^b- 757   ne wæs his drohtoð þǣr / swylce hē on ealderdagum
                        ǣr gemētte.

739 - 794^a   nē his līfdagas   lēoda ǣnigum / nytte tealde.

                        These three quotes refer to the fate of Grendel
                        before and during his fight with Beowulf in
                        Heorot, all of them concerned with his lack of
                        a future.

821^b- 823^a   wiste þē geornor / þæt his aldres wæs ende
                        gegongen, dōgera dægrīm.

                        Here Grendel is aware that his time has run out.

884^b- 885   Sigemunde gesprong / æfter dēaðdæge dōm unlȳtel,

                        This reference is to the death and posthumous
                        fame of Sigemund, told by the minstrel in Heorot
                        after Beowulf's victory over Grendel.

1061^b-1062 Fela sceal gebīden / lēofes ond lāþes sē þe longe
                        hēr on ðyssum windagum   worolde brūceð!

The series of quotes I have just given begins and ends with a
general comment on man's fate, but the others (with the exception of the reference to Sigemund) are all connected to
the death of Grendel, to his timely demise.

         Part two opens with the history of the dragon's hoard
and the Survivor's Lament, upon which our first quote is a
comment.

2268^b-2270^a   unblīðe hwearf / dæges ond nihtes, oð ðæt dēaðes
                        wylm hrān æt heortan.

                        The solitary man restlessly waits until death

claims him.

2341^b-2342   Sceolde lǣndaga / æþeling ǣrgōd ende gebīdan

2399^b-2400   oð ðone ānne dæg / þē hē wið wyrme gewegan

               sceolde

               Both of these are ominous, concerning Beowulf's

               approaching fight with the dragon which will

               lead to his death.

2590^b-2591^a   swā sceal ǣghwylc / ālǣtan lǣndagas.

               Although a general comment on the transitory

               nature of existence, this immediately follows

               a remark to the effect that Beowulf will die

               soon.

2725^b-2726   wisse hē gearwe / þæt hē dæghwīla gedrogen

               hæfde

               Beowulf recognizes his imminent death here,

               which he puts into words in the next quote:

2797 -2798   þæs ðe ic mōste mīnum lēodum

               ǣr swyltdæge swylc gestrȳnan.

3069   Swā hit oð dōmes dæg dīope benemdon

               Here the curse which caused Beowulf's death is

               mentioned and the series concludes with the

               (conjectural) quote from the woman's lament,

               concerning evil days to come.

3153   þæt hīo hyre hearmdagas hearde ondrēde

    In part one, the first general remark concerning death

is followed by Beowulf's boast. The next three are narrative

comments on Grendel's coming death, followed by Grendel's

own recognition of that fact. Part two opens with the fate
of the last survivor, followed again by three narrative comments on Beowulf's fate to come and then the hero's acknow-
ledgement which is put into words. The series concludes with
an explanation of the curse and an ominous prediction. The
number and the patterns of these two series of references to
mortality, first concerning Grendel then Beowulf, are remarkably alike. Between the two of them falls the single reference of this type to Grendel's mother. These references all
use the idea of day (or days) as a point at which death comes
-- time has run out -- or at which evil will come. The idea
of finishing or ending a limit of days -- a man's life -- is
obvious.

"Niht" and its compounds, associated closely with the
three monsters with whom Beowulf has to contend, are frequently
used in a qualitative manner. There is the direct reference
to danger in Beowulf's night-battles with sea-serpents (422;
547; 575); there is the dark of the night in which Grendel
approaches Heorot, the hall of light ("sweartum," 167;
"deorcum," 275; "wanre," 702); there is the "nihtbealwa" (193)
of Grendel's ravages, and the dragon which "nihtes flēogeð"
(2273). "ǣfen" has similar associations: after the feast to
celebrate Grendel's destruction, the men in Heorot little
knew what would befall them "syþðan ǣfen cwōm" (1235), and
the dragon impatiently waits "oð ðæt ǣfen cwōm" (2303) so
that it can begin its attacks. Neither "dæg" or "niht" have
the brilliant qualities that "jor" and "nuit" often possess

in the Roland, although affective, emotional overtones are frequent.

Another aspect of both "dæg" and "niht" -- almost absent from the Roland[16]-- is that of duration, although it is not objective duration. That is to say, it is bound up with action and the emphasis is on the length of the time; there is also a connection with negative feelings, evil or danger. Grendel holds the moors "sinnihte" (161) -- 'in endless night'; Unferth warns Beowulf of his fate if he dares to stand guard "nihtlongne" (528); Beowulf reports to Hygelac that they feasted "andlangne dæg" (2115), unaware of the threat of Grendel's mother; Beowulf's men waited "morgenlongne dæg" (2894) for the result of the dragon-fight.

We have discussed at some length the narrative patterning of Beowulf and the associations of times of the daily cycle with emotion. Now let us see if there is a regular recurrence of the parts of the day and if phrases function as indicators of beginning or ending of action. Dawn and nightfall, as with Roland, are obvious points to consider.

The daily sequence of light and dark is used in Beowulf but since the poem shifts so frequently in its time-setting the sequence of narrative action blocks does not match the daily cycle as closely as does that of the Roland. Another important point -- already demonstrated -- is that a great deal of action takes place at night in Beowulf. In the Roland, battle ceases at nightfall, the army sleeps and perhaps Charlemagne dreams. But all Beowulf's adversaries are creatures

of the dark, so that nightfall marks the beginning of some
of the most important actions of the poem -- the onslaughts
of Grendel and his mother, Beowulf's battle with Grendel,
and the depredations of the dragon. Grendel's mother and the
dragon are both defeated during the daylight.

PATTERN OF NIGHT AND DAY IN BEOWULF

Line	Quote		Time of Day
115	syþðan niht becōm	Grendel's first attack	NIGHTFALL
126	on ūhtan mid ǣrdæge	Results are visible	DAWN
645-646	[Hroðgar] sēcean wolde / ǣfenræste	Knows Grendel's schedule	NIGHTFALL
731	ǣr þon dæg cwōme	Grendel acts at night	NIGHT
837	Ðā wæs on morgen	Grendel's arm visible	DAWN
1235	syþðan ǣfen cwōm	Grendel's mother will come	NIGHTFALL
1311	Samod ǣrdæge	Results are visible	DAWN
2303	oð ðæt ǣfen cwōm	Dragon will act	NIGHTFALL
2320	ǣr dæges hwīle	Dragon returns home	DAWN

This pattern concerns the main actions of the narrative. The four cycles of Night/Day cover the four episodes of agression: the first one, Grendel's initial attack; the second, Grendel's attack and defeat by Beowulf; the third, the unexpected attack by Grendel's mother; and the fourth, the dragon's first ravages. Other references, outside the main group of events, follow:

Line	Quote		Time of Day
413-414	siððan æfenlēoht / ... beholen weorþeð	Beowulf says that Heorot became empty	NIGHTFALL
484-485	on morgentīd / ... þonne dæge līxte	Hroðgar tells of Grendel's first attacks: results visible	DAWN
518	on morgentīd	Unferth tells of Breca	DAWN
565	on mergenne	Beowulf tells of Breca: results visible	DAWN
1077	syþðan morgen cōm	Scop tells of Finn: slaughter visible	DAWN
2072-2073	Syððan heofones gim / glād ofer grundas	Beowulf tells Hygelac of Grendel's attack	NIGHTFALL
2103	syððan mergen cōm	results: gift giving	DAWN
	(This corresponds to 731 and 837)		
2116	oð ðæt niht becwōm	Beowulf tells Hygelac of Grendel's mother's attack	NIGHTFALL
2124	syððan mergen cōm	Death of Æschere becomes visible	DAWN
	(This corresponds to 1235 and 1311)		
2939	on mergenne	Ongentheow's threats for the morning	NIGHT
2942	somod ærdæge	Hygelac armies to save Geats	DAWN

Almost always there is a connection, both of action and of time, between nightfall and dawn. Action at night is followed by recognition at dawn, and because the initiator of the action is frequently one of the creatures of the dark, nightfall is <u>necessary</u> for the action to begin. The logical relation is made clear by such words as 'when', 'until', 'before' ("syððan"; "oð ðæt"; "ær"). The time at which the results of the night's work become visible is actually precisely by 'at' ("on"; "samod"). The two descriptions of Beowulf's swimming match with Breca, although they do not apparently begin at nightfall, occupy "seofon niht" (517) according to Unferth and at least "fīf nihta" (545) according to Beowulf, who emphasizes the "nīpende niht" (547). The attack on Finn obviously occurred at night since the damage was plain for Hildeburh to see in the morning.

The pattern of Night-Dawn // Action-Reaction is almost perfectly consistent: those "sets" which occur among the "elaborations" are the least complete (the two Breca descriptions; the Finn episode; the battle at Ravenswood). Perhaps this helps to confirm our previous findings that the elaborations have different time-frames from those of the narrative -- it seems of less importance to stress the natural cycle of day within these ornamental elaborations, which are almost always in <u>past</u> time.

The structure of <u>Beowulf</u> in non-linear in narrative form as has been pointed out by many critics. It is also non-linear in time, with the main sequence of action continually broken into "elaborations" which add depths to the plot but which involve time shifts. The references to 'day' and 'night' are used in some ways similarly to the way they are used in the Roland: many have little to do with the passage of time within the narrative, but concern the end of a man's life -- his time has come to its inevitable conclusions. Unlike some instances in the Roland, there are very few references in Beowulf to the quality of the day itself, removed from the events which take place in it. In the Roland, the changes in the daily cycle (i.e., dawn and nightfall) are noted but separate from the action, whereas in Beowulf, as has been shown, there is an explicit grammatical and logical connection between these changes and the events of the poem, and one period of time is contrasted with another. The whole of Beowulf seems to be infused with a contrast in the happiness, virtue and wealth of one time as opposed to the misery, evil and poverty of another.

Let us now look at the Old Norse poems to see how their structure functions in relation to time and its indications. As we pointed out in an earlier chapter, Atlakviða contains no words indicating either duration of time nor any points in the cycle of day or night: stanza thirty contains "sól inni suðhǫllo" -- 'the southward-curving sun', which may refer to morning, but that is all. It is impossible, therefore to try to link the patterns of the narrative to the pattern of time since the latter cannot be discerned. But perhaps the narrative structure may reveal a style or pattern that is of interest to our investigation.

We agree with Dronke that "the poem is ordered in three great acts," but it is possible to develop that idea further in the light of what was said about the structure of the Roland. The action of Atlakviða can be divided into four parts by the journeys the characters undertake, and, as with the Roland, the journeys frame the dramatic events and are outside time.

Pattern of Narrative in Atlakviða

JOURNEY OF KNEFRØÐR

Stanza	Content	Dronke's 'Acts'
2-12	Challenge and response	I
13	JOURNEY TO ATLI	
14-28	Arrival and capture; death of Hogni	
29-31	JOURNEY TO HEATH	II
32	Death of Gunnarr	
33	JOURNEY FROM HEATH	
34-44	Guðrún's revenge; death of boys and Atli	III

Within none of the narrative sections, however, is there any connection with any part of the natural time cycle.

In spite of the intensity of the action and what Dronke calls the "compressed ... enigmatic vocabulary" (p. 43), considering the brevity of the poem there is much elaboration in the forms of lists, repetition, and description, as well as comments on past behavior and prophecies of the future.

For example, the list of treasure, property and weapons given
by Knefrøðr as inducement to the brothers to visit Atli (stanzas 4 and 5) is paralleled by that which Gunnarr enumerates to indicate the pointlessness of the offer (stanza 7). An idea
represented in the first half of a stanza may be repeated in
the second half in different words:

Stanza

11/1-4 Úlfr mun ráða ... ef Gunnars missir

11/5-6 birnir blakfialler bíta ... ef Gunnarr né
kømerat

['The wolf shall rule ... if Gunnar is lost

'the black-skinned bears bite ... if Gunnar

does not return']

The two scenes in which a man's heart is cut out and
offered to Gunnarr are, not surprisingly, close in structure
and words:

Skáro þeir hiarta ...	et til hiarta skáro ...
blóðugt ok á bioð logðo	Blóðugt þat á bioð logðo
ok báro þat fyr Gunnar	ok báro fyr Gunnar
Stanza 22/1; 3-4	Stanza 24/2; 6-7
Þá kvað þat Gunnarr,	Mærr kvað þat Gunnarr,
gumna dróttinn:	geir-Niflungr:
'Hér hefi ek hiarta	'Hér hefi ek hiarta
Hialla ins blauða,	Hǫgna ins froekna,
ólíkt hiarta	ólíkt hiarta
Hǫgna ins froekna,	Hialla ins blauða,
er miǫk bifax,	er lítt bifax

er á bióði liggr --	er á bióði liggr --
bifðiz hálfo mierr,	bifðiz svági miǫk,
er í briósti lá.	þá er í briósti lá.
Stanza 23	Stanza 25
They cut the heart ...	as they cut the heart ..
Bleeding and laid it on a platter	bleeding, they laid it on the platter
and brought that before Gunnarr	and brought it before Gunnarr
Stanza 22/1; 3-4	Stanza 24/2; 6-7
Then said Gunnarr,	Noble Gunnarr spoke,
leader of men	the spear of Niflung,
"Here I have the heart	"Here I have the heart
of Hialli the coward	of Hogni the brave
unlike the heart	unlike the heart
of Hogni the brave,	of Hialli the coward,
it quivers much	it quivers little
as it lies on the platter --	as it lies on the platter --
it quivered twice as much	it quivered much less
when it lay in his breast.	when it lay in his breast.

The description of Atli's fortress occupies the whole of stanza 14, a stanza of double length, delaying the arrival scene, the meeting of Guðrún and her brothers.

Much of the poem (twenty stanzas out of forty-four) is direct speech, and of this a large amount does not affect the action but comments on it as do the boasts of the Saracens before the battle in the Roland in parallel laisses, such as laisses 73-78. These comments, it seems to me, frequently

act to increase the emotional intensity of the scene in which

they occur. In stanza eight, Hogni's discovery of the wolf's

hair twisted in the ring from Guðrún, and its ominous meaning,

is referred to twice:

'Hvat hyggr þú brúði bendo,	'What do you think the lady meant
þá er hon okr baug sendi	when she sent us a ring
varinn váðom heiðingia?	wrapped in the heath-ranger's coat?
Hygg ek, at hon vornuð byði.	I think she offered us a warning.
Hár fann ek heiðingia	I found a hair of the heath-ranger
riðit í hring rauðom.	twisted round the red ring.
Ylfskr er vegr okkarr	Our way is wolfish
at ríða ørindi.'	if we ride on this journey.'

I have also just mentioned stanza eleven in which the first

and second halves repeat the same ominous prophecy in dif-

ferent words -- in stanza sixteen there is a triple repetition

of what should have been done. At the moment Guðrún meets her

brothers she tells them that, having refused to heed her

warning, they ought at least to have armed themselves:

'Betr hefðir þú, bróðir,	'You would have done better, brother,
at þú í brynio foerir ...	if you had come in mail coats
Sætir þú í sǫðlom	You should have stayed in the saddle
sólheiða daga ...	through sunlit days ...

en Atli siálfan   while Atli himself

léter þú í ormgarð koma.' you whould have brought
                           into the snake-pit.'

There is not the closeness of phrasing which some of
the _Roland_ passages have, but the effect is the same -- the
audience is compelled to concentrate attention on the emotion
of the scene. There is an important difference, however,
which is that here the present situation is contrasted with
the situation as it ought to have been. A similar use of the
repitition of an idea, but with reference to the future, occurs
in stanza twenty-seven. Gunnarr has just made certain of
Hogni's death and tells Atli that the secret of the family
treasure will die with him:

'Rin skal ráða   'The Rhine shall be master

rógmálmi skatna,   of the metal of men's
                          strife

[á] sú in áskunna,   the god-sprung river rule

arfi Niflunga   the inheritance of the
                          Niflunger.

í veltanda vatni   In rolling waters rather

lýsaz valbaugar,   shall the foreign rings
                          glint

heldr en á hǫndom   than that gold should shine

gull skíni Húna bǫrnom.' on the Huns' children's
                          hands!'

Guðrún's announcement to Atli, in stanzas thirty-seven and
thirty-eight, that he has just eaten the flesh of their sons
contains two emotional elements -- the horror of cannibalism
and the loss of the children. Each emotion is stressed by

repetition in a way similar to that of the examples:

'Sona hefir þinna	'You have your own sons'
sverða deilir,	--giver of swords--
hiǫrto hrædreyog	bleeding hearts from their bodies
við hunang of tuggin.	chewed with honey.
Melta knátto, móðugr,	You are digesting, proud one,
manna valbráðir,	slaughtered human meat,
eta at ǫlkrásom	eating it as ale-morsels,
ok í ondugi at senda.'	sending it to the high seats.'

'Kallaraðu síðan	'You will not again call
til kniá þinna	to your knee
Erp né Eitil,	Erpr or Eitill,
ǫlreifa tvá--	both merry with feasting--
séraðu síðan	you will not see again
í seti miðio	at the center of the dais
gullz me lendr	the bounteous princes
geira skepta,	fitting shafts to their spears,
mana meita	clipping manes,
né mara keyra.'	or cantering their horses.'

These examples demonstrate that the apparent speed of
the action of <u>Atlakviða</u> is in fact delayed at dramatic moments
and the emotions heightened by repitition related to the
emotion conveyed by the action: Hogni's repeat of his discovery
of the wolf-hair twisted in the ring is the deciding factor

in the Nibelung's journey. Gunnarr's ominous remarks before
departing, the meeting with Guðrún, the death of Hogni,
Gunnarr's defiance of Atli, and Guðrún's announcement to Atli
are the emotional peaks of the poem. In each case the emotion
is emphasized by repetition in direct speech by the main
character concerned.

Like that of the Roland and Beowulf then, the action goes
forward, pauses, then goes forward again. The pauses, the
elaborations, are shorter than those in the other poems but
then Atlakviða is much shorter than both Roland and Beowulf.
But whereas in the similar laisses of the Roland the repetitions
almost always take place within the time-frame of the poem,
in Atlakviða there is usually a connection between present or
recent action and (usually) a future event:

Stanza

8	"Our way is [i.e., will be] wolfish if we ride ..."
11	"The wolf shall ride ... if Gunnarr is lost"
16	"You would have done better if you had come in mail-coats"
27	[now Hogni is dead] "The Rhine shall be master ..."
38	[now Erp and Eitill are dead] "You will not call again to your knee ..."

This is similar to the elaborations of Beowulf in that
there are temporal references, but different in that in
Atlakviða the connection is a causal one, that is, present
action leads conditionally to future results: in Beowulf
present events are opposed to those of the past, but there is

no causal relationship. Atlakviða as a whole is not explicitly set in a distant past, as is Beowulf, but the events are related as if they would have occurred within the poet's or his audience's lifetime; that is to say, the temporal setting of the narrative is not contrasted with that of the poet and his audience.

Atlamál differs in many ways from its earlier analogue; most obvious at first is what one might call the domestication of the story. There is no mention of Huns, Burgundians, fabulous treasures, nor journeys across Mirkwood to the Rhine. Atli lives on a farm, not in a splendid castle, and the message from Guðrún is a written one, not the symbolic wolf's hair wrapped around a ring. Motives are down-to-earth, comparable to those one finds in the Icelandic family sagas. Atli accuses Guðrún of cheating him of his wealth and causing trouble in the family to which Guðrún retorts that he had killed her mother for gain and starved her cousin to death.

The narrative is composed with quite a different emphasis from that in Atlakviða. Here, a brief introduction is followed by the journey of Atli's messengers (stanza four), the discovery of the distorted message and two sets of ominous dreams (5-34), and the journey to Atli's farm (34-36). The battle and the deaths of Hogni and Gunnarr occupy almost thirty stanzas (38-64), and the rest of the poem includes long interpretive dialogues between Atli and Guðrún interspersed with Guðrún's terrible vengeance, the attack on Atli and his death.

As with Atlakviða, roughly half of Atlamál is direct
speech, but there is little of the retarding effect of the
balanced repetitions and prophetic statements of the earlier
poem. Kostbera's warning to Hogni takes the form of a sequence
of dream images -- a devouring fire, a terrifying bear, and a
bloody eagle (15; 16; 18). Glaumvor's to Gunnarr is similar
-- she dreams of a gallows, of serpents, a bloody sword, and
a raging river (21; 22; 24).

The attitude toward time is also different, both implied
and direct. I have already referred to the opening stanza
which places the story in the distant past. Other past references are those just mentioned in the motives for the action
of the poem -- past acts of both Atli and Guðrún are stated
as the causes for the present hatred brought to the surface in
the climax of the poem. As she prepares her two sons for their
death, Guðrún tells them that she has long wished to cure them
of old age (75). While Atlakviða, then, refers to future
results of present acts, Atlamál relates past causes of present
dissension.

Both points of time and duration are connected to the
action of Atlamál, although not to any great extent. Bedtime
is followed by dreams which are explained on waking:

Sæing fóro síðan ... Dreymði dróttláta ... hon

réð vakna

('Then they went to bed ... the queen dreamed ...
explained on waking' [10/1, 3 6])

The act of rising is connected to sunrise in stanza 27:

Lito, er lýsti / létoz þeir fúsir / allir upp rísa

('They saw dawn was coming, said they were all
  eager to rise')

The deaths of Hogni and Gunnarr take place "dags var held
snemma" ('the day was rather early' [64/2]) and Atli also remarks on this in the next sentence: "'Morginn er nú'" ('it is
morning now' [65/5]); a further reference to this is made by
Guðrún in her speech of vengeance when she says, "'Morgin mér
saðir ... nú er ok aptann'" ('You said to me it was morning
... now it is evening' [78]).

We might, then, set up a pattern in which time of day is
connected to action:

Time of Day	Stanza	Action
NIGHTFALL	10	Bedtime followed by dreams which are described on waking
DAWN	27	Arising
EARLY MORNING	64	Hogni and Gunnarr are killed
	65	
	78	Reference in Guðrún's revenge speech, 'then it was morning'
EVENING	78	'now it is evening'

There are not precise or frequent but the concept of a connection between time of day and action is present, unlike the
situation in the Roland in which one followed the other but
was not connected either grammatically or logically. There
is no suggestion that these points of time follow each other
in a linked sequence.

Duration is also indicated in Atlamál, though again only

once or twice. The conclusion of the preparation of the feast, the preparation of beer and the killing of the boys so their skulls could be used as drinking cups, was discussed in a previous chapter. There is a vague indication that several -- perhaps many -- days passed between the death of Gunnarr and Hogni, and the funeral feast is expressed by Guðrún's remark, "'Svaf ek miok sialden'" ('I have rarely slept [78/1]), and the journey to Atli's farm takes some time at least: "Litlo ok lengra" ('A short time later' [36/1]).

But the battle itself, the climactic action of the poem, is stressed by the duration connected with it:

> Morgin mest vágo
>
> unz miðian dag líddi,
>
> ótto alla
>
> ok ǫndurðan dag.
>
> (50/1-4)

('They fought most in the morning, past the middle of the day, through the first hours and the forenoon.') The battle is not a major conflict since there are less than forty men included altogether, but it continues till the afternoon. A measure of the strength and valor of Guðrún's brothers and their comrades is not only the number of Atli's men they killed, but the time which they filled with their heroic deeds. Endurance within a temporal structure is connected to moral and heroic worth.

The linearity of style and structure, the different attitudes toward past and present, and the concept of duration in Atlamál would all seem to indicate a cultural context

qualitatively different from that of Atlakviða, once in which
the influence of a literary tradition is possibly beginning
to appear.

The patterns of time and narrative we have considered
in this chapter vary from the extremely paratactic, repetitive,
discontinuous Roland to the much more linear Atlamál. In the
Roland, time is cyclic, qualitative, and closely linked to
action within the narrative, while in Beowulf there is a strong
linear sense of time and the "digressions" jump backwards and
forwards in time.   Atlakviða is closer to the Roland in
that the journeys are outside time. There is also repetitive
structure similar to that of the Roland but an absence of
references to the cycle of day and night. Atlamál is stylistically more linear than Atlakviða, and the feeling of time
is also less cyclical -- past quarrels have caused present
feud -- and events have a more definite duration. In the next
chapter we shall return to the later texts.

NOTES

[1]See Joseph J. Duggan, The Song of Roland: Formulaic Style and Poetic Craft, p. 63; Pierre le Gentil, La Chanson de Roland (Paris: Hatier-Boivin, 1955), p. 90; Jean Rychner, La Chanson de Geste: essai sur l'art épique des jongleurs (Geneva: Droz, 1955), pp. 38-29; Fern Farnham, "Romanesque Design in the Chanson de Roland," Romance Philology, 18 (1964), 143-164.

[2]J. J. Duggan, The Song of Roland: Formulaic Style and Poetic Craft, pp. 64-68.

[3]Jean Rychner, La Chanson de Geste: essai sur l'art épique des jongleurs, Chapter III.

[4]Joseph L. Anderson and Donald Richie, The Japanese Film (New York: Grove Press, 1960), pp. 272-73.

[5]Milman Parry, "The Distinctive Character of Enjambment in Homeric Verse," TAPA, 55 (1929), 200-220; Albert B. Lord, "Homer and Huso III," TAPA, 79 (1948), 113-124; James Botopoulos, "Parataxis in Homer," TAPA, 80 (1949), 1-23.

[6]Albert Lord, The Singer of Tales, p. 54.

[7]See the first chapter for a discussion of the idea of the connection between alphabetic writing and logical, linear thought.

[8]Erich Auerbach, Mimesis, pp. 2, 5, 3.

[9]J. R. R. Tolkien, "Beowulf: The Monsters and the Critics," in The Beowulf Poet, (ed.) Donald K. Fry (Englewood Cliffs, New Jersey: Prentice-Hall, 1968), pp. 154-66.

[10]Joan Blomfield, "The Style and Structure of Beowulf,"

in The Beowulf Poet, pp. 57-65; Adrien Bonjour, The Digressions
in Beowulf (Oxford: Blackwells, 1950); A. G. Brodeur, The Art
of Beowulf (Berkeley and Los Angeles: University of California
Press, 1959); K. Sisam, The Structure of Beowulf (Oxford:
Clarendon, 1965); J. Nist, "The Structure of Beowulf," P.M.A.
S.A.L., 43 (1958), 307-14; John Leyerle, "The Interlace
Structure of Beowulf," University of Toronto Quarterly, 37
(1967), 1-17; Adeline Courtney Bartlett, The Larger Rhetorical
Patterns in Anglo-Saxon Poetry (New York: Columbia University
Press, 1935).

[11]Adrien Bonjour, "The use of anticipation in Beowulf,"
Review of English Studies, 16 (1940), 291-99.

[12]Alain Renoir, "Point of View and Design for Terror,"
in The Beowulf Poet, pp. 154-66.

[13]K. Sisam, The Structure of Beowulf, p. 4.

[14]Edward B. Irving, Jr. "The Pattern of Until," in A
Reading of Beowulf (New Haven: Yale University Press, 1968),
pp. 31-42.

[15]See Herbert G. Wright, "Good and Evil; Light and Darkness; Joy and Sorrow in Beowulf," Review of English Studies,
n.s., 8 (1957), 1-11.

[16]Except at line 1780, where Ganelon criticizes Roland
for hunting a single hare for the whole day: "Pur un sul levre
vait tute jur cornant."

Chapter V

PATTERNS OF TIME AND NARRATIVE: LATER TEXTS

In this chapter we shall discuss Yvain, Sir Gawain and
the Green Knight, Gunnlaugs Saga, and "The Shipman's Tale" with
respect to patterns of narrative and of time in order to discover if there is a qualitative difference in this regard between the earlier texts of the last chapter and these later
ones.

We have already pointed out that the text of Yvain is
seen at once to be arranged differently on the page than is
that of the Roland. Chrétien's poem consists of rhyming
couplets with no obvious breaks, and the style is linear --
at least in comparison with the Roland. Hypotaxis rather than
parataxis is the rule,[1] and there is a sense of more or less
continuous time in which past, present, and future can be
distinguished. But how are the events of the narrative related to one another -- do they succeed each other in a simple
linear arrangement? How are they linked to one another and
what is their connection, if any, to a temporal continuum?

There are two or three approaches by which we can try to
break up Yvain into separate parts. The poem tells chiefly of
a knight who undertakes a series of adventures during a long
journey, the purpose of which is not to arrive at a particular
geographical location but to experience and overcome difficulties by which he may regain his honor and his wife. His
journeys become more and more specific geographically and
motivationally.

We can, then, try to separate one adventure from the next and see if the journey between serves to separate or to link the two. But immediately we run into difficulties, since, as was implied above, the journey and the adventures are often almost one and the same thing. It also becomes quickly obvious that more than one adventure may be taking place at the same time -- we may have to keep in mind that Yvain is in one place while one or more secondary characters occupy the forefront of the action. The hero himself may set out on one mission but become involved in another so that there is a question in the reader's mind (and in the hero's) as to whether he will be able to complete his original task -- the journey may thus be used to increase the reader's interest in the action. Simultaneous events are handled with some skill.

Since neither the journeys nor the adventures can be consistently used as a method of dividing the narrative into distinct components, we may try a thematic approach. Concerning the character of Yvain, there are two major divisions of the poem: the first is from the moment he leaves Arthur's court secretly to undertake the adventure of the fountain to the time when he lives as a wild beast in the forest; the second is from the beginning of his mental and physical recovery to his reconciliation first with the world of chivalry at court and then with his beloved wife, Laudine.

Another approach to the partition of the narrative is to look at the actual manuscript to see if the scribe himself makes any divisions in the text. In the Guiot copy, which is

used for Mario Roques' edition, there are two different kinds
of ornamental letters, indicated in the Roques' edition by
indentation. The "initiales ornées" appear at the beginning
of the narrative (an especially large and elaborate example),
at lines 2331, 4543, and a space is left for one at 6143.
These occupy six lines except for the first and the space at
6143 which is four. There are also sixty-eight "capitales
montantes" which extend for two lines or more.

We shall now examine the text with these different approaches, beginning with the large themes to see how they can
or cannot be used in an analysis of the narrative structure
of Yvain, and then try to relate them to any patterning of
time which may parallel the narrative.

The downfall of Yvain involves several stages -- first,
the reader is aware thet Yvain has forgotten his promise:

> ...tant demorer
>
> que toz li anz fu trespassez
>
> et de tot l'autre encor assez,
>
> tant que a la mi aost vint
>
> (2678-81)

The promise was to return by the feast of St. John the Baptist
which is June 24th, so it is clear that Yvain is long overdue.
We are then given evidence of Yvain's pride since we are told
that he and Gawain never go to the court but that the king has
to come to them. Next Yvain begins to think about his lady
and his leave-taking and realizes that "covant manti li avoit /
et trespassez estoit li termes" (2702-03). His tears begin to

flow, a damsel appears who exposes Yvain's failure, he is be-
reft of speech, and the damsel leaves. Yvain wishes to be
far away, his actions follow his words, and "lors se li monte
uns torbeillons el chief, si grant que li forsane" (2806-07).
He wanders aimlessly til his senses return enough for him to
borrow and use a bow and arrows to kill game, and then a
hermit leaves bread and water for him in return for which he
leaves some of his game for the hermit. One day Yvain is
found naked and asleep by two damels and their lady; he is
recognized, anointed while asleep with healing ointment, and
some clothes are left for him. He wakes and has regained his
senses.

From the point where the reader recognizes Yvain's failure
to the moment when the hero wakes and recovers "son san et son
mimoire" (3015) is more than three hundred lines, but it is
difficult to say precisely where the break between "downfall"
and "recovery" can be identified. One could argue that it is
where the reader first realizes Yvain's failure, or where
Yvain himself recognizes his fault. In either case, though,
the following three hundred lines must be seen as a link between the two thematic divisions. One could also argue that
the point at which Yvain's fault is made public marks the
nadir of his moral standing, or the lines in which his loss
of sanity, his stripping off his clothes (signs of rank), takes
place. Does his contact with the boy from whom he borrows the
bow and arrows, or the wordless exchange of food with the
hermit mark the beginning of his reintegration into human

society and the slow recovery of his former rank? But his
recovery comprises several different components: first there
is his "san et mimoire," then the recovery of his physical
powers which the damsel tells him will take "jusqu'a quinzainne"
(3078). His moral revival may be said to begin at the moment
he asks the same damsel "se vos avez besoing de moi" (3075),
but this itself has two separate elements -- his return to his
own name and to Arthur's court which is completed by his duel
with Gawain, and his forgiveness by Laudine at the very end
of the poem: "Or a mes sire Yvains sa pes" (6879).

The flight of Yvain from the court in his madness is
quite unlike the journeys which transport Charlemagne and
Marsile in the _Roland_. Yvain has morally erred and his literally senseless wandering is a concrete image of the error of
his ways -- he is an errant knight in more ways than one. His
meanderings are an essential part of the action and do not
serve to frame or set off one part of the action from another.

The division of the poem according to "downfall" and
"recovery," then, depends on which particular aspect of the
narrative the reader is most concerned with -- it is the
reader who makes such a decision, not the author. Nor is the
scribe of any help to us, since the only capital occurs in
the middle of the damsel's accusatory speech, when she shifts
from an address directed to the court in which Yvain's behavior and that of Laudine are described to one directed at
Yvain himself: "Yvain, n'a mes cure de toi / me dame" (2769-
70). This marks a change in the audience for which the speech

is intended, but not a break in the sequence of events.

Let us look at the adventures, journeys, and 'paragraphs' (marked by capitals) to see where they do -- and do not -- correspond.

After Chrétien sets the scene -- the feast of Pentecost at Arthur's court "a Carduel en Gales" (7) at which there is much gaiety -- we are told that Calogrenant is telling an story, and following some typically insulting remarks by Kay, the story begins: "Il m'avint plus a de set anz..." (173). Calogrenant says that he was travelling in the search of adventures "si come chevaliers doit estre" (177) -- the purpose of his journey is adventure. After his defeat by the knight of the fountain, he returned to court: "Ensi alai, ensi reving" (577); his speech, adventure, and his journey all begin and end together, but there are no corresponding opening or closing paragraphs. This story, of course, is a tale within a tale, so one would naturally expect it to end with its author's telling of it.

The interest of Yvain (and of the king) is aroused and Yvain leaves secretly as soon as he can: "Mes sire Yvains de la court s'anble" (723), and the scribe favors us with a capital. Yvain follows the same course as Calogrenant except that he defeats Esclados, pursues him to the castle and after an eventful few days marries the widow, Laudine. The journey ends at the castle but the adventure surely does not conclude until the wedding. Even Yvain's marriage does not mark a break in the action since we are told that the celebrations last "jusqu'a la voille / que li rois vint a la mervoille / de la fontainne" (2173-75). One of the reasons given for the hasty marriage is the imminence of Arthur's arrival, so we have had to keep in mind that while Yvain was preparing for his wedding, the court was already on its way.

Kay begs for the chance to challenge the guardian of the fountain (Yvain, of course), and is suitably rewarded for his temerity. Yvain identifies himself and invites the king to stay at the castle where there is a great welcome.

The second "initiale ornée" marks the point at which the people of the castle come out to welcome the king: "Encontre le roi de Bretaingne / vont tuit sor granz chevax d'Espaingne" (2331-32), but the arrival cannot be said to be completed at least before Arthur quickly dismounts to avoid having Laudine hold his stirrup for him: "si descendi lues qu'il la vit" (2379).

The celebrations at the castle last a week, during which Gawain persuades Yvain to join him at the tournaments to show the world he has not lost his valor just because he is now a married man. Yvain receives permission from Laudine and promises to return, with the results we have already seen. His departure is marked by a capital at line 2641: "Mes sire Yvains molt a enviz / est de s'amie departiz."

The 'downfall' of Yvain lasts at least until he recovers "son san et son mimoire" at line 3015. There seems to be no obvious logical division of the narrative into separate episodes but rather a continuous sequence of action.

With the beginning of the adventures which Yvain undertakes to restore his reputation, however, the narrative becomes more complex. The lady of Norison, who has looked after
Yvain, is attacked by the Count Alier. Yvain defeats the
enemy of his benefactress and as soon as everything is arranged
to her satisfaction he asks permission to depart:

> Quant ces choses furent asises
>
> ensi com a la dame sist,
>
> mes sire Yvains congié an quist
>
> (3310-12)

Even though he is begged to stay "or se mist a la voie arriere /
et leissa molt la dame iriee" (3320-21). The transition here
is marked by a capital: "Mes sire Yvains pansis chemie" (3337),
and in this case the beginning of a journey also initiates a
new adventure, that of the lion. After a night in the forest,
Yvain and the lion continue to travel together, "Au main s'an
alerent ensanble" (3479) and spend the next two weeks wandering
until by chance they come upon the magic fountain. One could
say that line 3479 begins the next journey and the next adventure
-- it is also emphasized by a capital. At the fountain Yvain
finds Lunete imprisoned and awaiting execution the following
day, and after promising to help her moves off to search for
a night's lodging which he duly finds. Here, however, a
complication develops since this is the castle threatened by
the giant Harpin. We have already seen how Chrétien uses the
efflux of time to heighten the drama of the narrative here,
but what we are now concerned with is the structural relations

of the narrative: the adventure of Lunete is interrupted here
for at least five hundred lines depending on whether one de-
cides that the Harpin adventure begins where Yvain sees the
castle at 3767 or when he enters it at 3797. Harpin falls at
4250 but Yvain is not able to escape the gratitude of those
he has saved until 4307; "Et maintenant que il s'an muet..."
This, in any case, is the point at which we return to Lunete's
predicament, with Yvain racing back to the chapel -- his
return journey marks a return to his primary obligation.

The struggle with Lunete's accusers finishes with Yvain
and his lion wounded and the villains condemned to the "meïsmes
mort ... que il ... a jugiee" (4568-69). This is the end of
the battle, but it is followed by a reconciliation between
Lunete and Laudine, and an ironic dialogue between Yvain and
Laudine in which the knight evades her questions, telling her
that he cannot rest until his lady is no longer angry with
him: Laudine, of course, only knows him as the Knight of the
Lion. This interlude which links the battle to Yvain's inevitable departure ends at line 4646: "Si s'an vet pansis et
detroiz." Notice that although a new journey starts here, the
line begins with a conjunction, making a grammatical connection
with what has immediately preceded it.

Chrétien leaves Yvain and the lion recuperating at a
convenient chateau -- "Jorx i sejorna ne sai quanz" (4694)
-- while he introduces us to the problems of the two daughters
of the Lady of Noire Espine who have gone to Arthur's court
in search of assistance in their dispute over their dead

father's property. The idea of simultaneity is here clearly
expressed. We follow the younger sister from the court
searching for the Knight of the Lion and see her falling sick,
and her friend gradually catching up with the hero she seeks.
This is another example of Chrétien using a rather modern
approach to a sequence of time and events to heighten suspense.
Adding to this is the time-limit of thirty days which the
king set for the younger sister to find a champion -- we have
to keep this in mind as we watch the pursuit through the
forest, and, after Yvain has been found, the entanglement of
another adventure, that of the castle of Pesme Aventure.

We have also been told that the younger sister reached
Arthur's court "s'avoit tierz jor que la reïne / ert de la
prison revenue" (4734-35) and that it was "an celui meïsmes
jor...fu venue la novele / del jaiant cruel" (4740-43). There
are, then, several elements of narrative which we must remember simultaneously, including a reference to a different story
Chrétien tells, that of his Lancelot.

The younger sister's departure from the court is marked
by a capital: "Ensi est an la queste antree" (4813), as is
the beginning of the Pesme Aventure episode when Yvain and
the damsel "ensi entr'aus deus chevalchierent" (5101), and
again as they enter the castle: "Ensi li portiers le semont"
(5179). Again, the use of "ensi" provides a link with
previous events.

The episode of Pesme Aventure ends at line 5803 after
Yvain has received and rejected the usual offers of wife and

property. He begins his journey to meet the younger daughter
of Noire Espine and, as her champion, proceeds to court: "Et
mes sire Yvains maintenant / de l'autre part se rachemine"
(5804-05).

The adventure of Noire Espine culminates in the duel
between Gawain and Yvain -- an inconclusive battle ending in
mutual recognition of the two knights and a rehabilitation of
Yvain's chivalric reputation at court. This ends part of
Yvain's personal quest, but does not coincide with the resolu-
tion of the Noire Espine disagreement which is decided by the
king.

While Yvain is recovering from his wounds, we are told
his plans for the future: "...il se partiroit / toz seus de
cort, et si iroit / a sa fontainne... / et s'i feroit tant
foudroier / et tant vanter, et tant plovoir, / que [sa dame]
covanroit feire a lui pes" (6605-13). As soon as he is strong
again, he acts: "Maintenant que mes sire Yvains / sant qu'il
fu gariz et sains, / si s'an parti" (6517-19). This is marked
by a capital.

The final part of his quest -- that of his reconciliation
with Laudine -- is straightforward structurally, with no in-
terruptions or elaborations. With the help of Lunete "a mes
sire Yvains sa pes; ...il est amez et chier tenuz / de sa dame,
et ele de lui (6789; 6794-95).

I believe I have convincingly demonstrated that the
narrative pattern of _Yvain_ is a complex one, essentially linear
but not separated easily into individual components. Scribal

divisions (the sixty-eight capitals) coincide in a few cases
(about a dozen) with other possible narrative divisions, such
as the beginnings of journeys or new adventures, themselves
extremely difficult to define. Many of these latter points
are grammatically connected to preceding narrative elements by
conjunctions or preposition, such as "et," "si," "ensi,"
"maintenant," which emphasize the continuity of the narrative,
prevent the reader's mind from wandering, and focus attention
upon what is to come.

The relation of the single adventures to one another is
sometimes that of simple sequence but also one which I shall
call "interleaved" rather than "interlaced" which is used by
Professor Vinaver.[2] In the later prose romances perhaps the
latter term is more appropriate. The following simplified
diagram will show what I mean.

THE ADVENTURES IN YVAIN

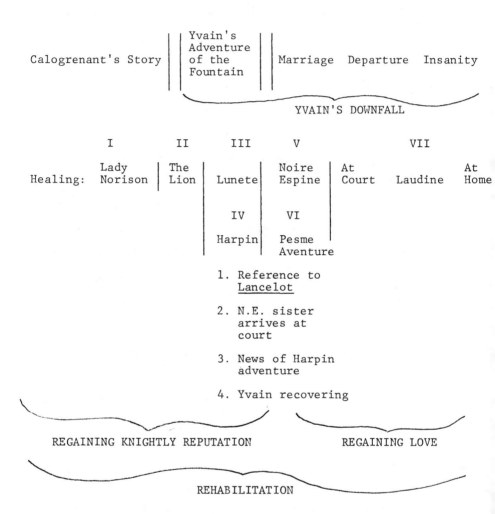

As Yvain approaches his goal, the reader has to keep more and more details in mind.

The Harpin episode is included within the boundaries of
the Lunete rescue, and the adventure of Pesme Aventure is within
that of Noire Espine. We also bear in mind Yvain's reputation
while the Noire Espine adventure begins, related as it is to
the Lancelot and to the recent defeat of Harpin. These events,
I suggest, are related by superimposition -- one being added
on to that which precedes it -- rather than the kind of intimate
intertwining which Vinaver described as characteristic of the
decorative art of the same period of history.

Let us now examine the words used which refer to time
and their arrangement to see is there are any changes in meaning
and implication and any relation to the complex narrative
patterns we have just described.

The longer periods of duration ("an"; "quinzainne";
"semainne") and the use of feast-days were discussed in Chapter
III, "Accounting for Time." We are left, then, with words
connected with the daily cycle of time and also those which
belong to the sequence of "yesterday-today-tomorrow" -- a
sequence not prominent in the Roland.

The most frequent of these time-words, as in the Roland,
is "jor" and its variants, with almost forty occurrences, followed by "nuit" (twenty-six), "matin" (six), "midi" (five),
and "vespree," "aube," "prime," "none," and "tierce" with one
or two occurrences each. "Demain" occurs thirteen times, "hui"
three, and "ier" once.

There is a great difference between the use of these
words in Yvain and in the Roland which is significant in terms

of our investigation; generally, in Yvain there is a definite change toward an objective sense of time and an increase of expectation -- there is a relative diminution of emotional and descriptive associations and the reader is pressed to consider what will happen next. In the Roland, it will be recalled, almost half of the occurrences of "jor" have emotional overtones, whereas in Yvain almost two-thirds are connected directly to the passage of time. This may be to a certain duration (e.g., "huit jorz apres la Saint Johan" [2576]; "par respit de trente jorz" [3685]; "jusqu'a quatorze jorz" [4797]), to a particular day (e.g., "le jor meïsmes" [2156]; "meïsmes jor" [4740]; "li derriens jorz" [5885]), or to the duration of a day or days (e.g., "li jor sont lonc" [1835]; "jorz i sejorna ne sai quanz" [4694]). Of the others, only one has emotional or esthetic connections ("li jorz fu baix" [5865]); the rest are related to habitual or repeated action, e.g., "chascun jor," "toz jurz," "trestoz les jorz." The concept of the 'flowing' of time is implied in the speech in which Yvain's perfidy is exposed: the damsel says that her lady marked off "trestoz les jorz et toz les tans" and refers to "les jorz qui vienent et qui vont" (2756 and 2761). Chrétien's efforts to increase the reader's interest in what will happen is shown in his use of "demain," which we shall discuss later.

Similarly, "nuit" represents both 'nightfall' and 'the duration of darkness', e.g., "Quant je ving la nuit a ostel" (561) and "Des nuiz grant partie veillons" (5314), but duration is far more frequently meant. There is one situation in which the discomfort of being benighted in a forest is stressed:

> Et la nuiz, et li bois le font
>
> grant enui, et plus le enuie
>
> que la nuiz, ne li bois, la pluie.

(4836-38)

The emphasis, however, is not on the fearfulness of the dark, but on the unpleasantness of the rain.

In the Roland we were able to show how the cycle of day and night is connected to the cyclic pattern of the narrative. Can we discover a similar relationship in Yvain? As with the question of accounting for time, we can answer "occasionally" -- at times Chrétien connects the events of his story with the natural cycle and at other times he does not. An important point to remember is that since the whole narrative rests on the framework of a journey it would be surprising if the author did not sometimes say that the hero began his day's journey in the morning and finished it in the evening. A modern traveller might say that on one day he found a convenient motel and spent the night there, left after breakfast and the following evening began to look for another place to stop -- in one case stressing the action and in the other mentioning the time of day, depending, perhaps, which is more significant in his recital.

In the earlier part of Yvain, where the narrative is related in a linear manner, Chrétien does not refer very much to the times of day at which events begin and conclude. But as the narrative becomes more complicated, these references become more frequent -- the placing of events in time is essential to the plot. So whereas in the Roland there seemed an almost mechanical relation between the beginning and ending of the action and the beginning and ending of the day, in Yvain the relationship between the sequence of events and the passage of time is an organic part of the story, and the author's and reader's attention becomes more directed to temporal sequence.

Calogrenant arrives at a castle, spends the night comfortably and leaves "lors que l'en pot le jor veoir" (270); after his defeat, he returns to spend "la nuit a ostel" (561). His return to court is not placed temporally. Yvain begins his journey, similarly spends the night and reaches the meadow guarded by the strange herdsman "l'andemain" (793). Not until after Yvain's downfall, his first adventure, and his rescue of the lion is there another point at which the time of day is related to action. The lion has just killed a deer for their dinner in the forest, and it is "pres de nuit" (3450). Yvain skins the deer, they both eat, sleep "tote la nuit" (3473) in the forest, and "au main s'an alerent ensanble" (3479).

The time at which Yvain meets the imprisoned Lunete is not mentioned and it is not until the hero and his feline companion search for and find a place to rest that we know Lunete is to be executed at midday next (3823; 3944; 3990). The necessity of the plot is reason enough for the statement that Yvain arose "a l'enjornee" (4023). The hero's swift dispatch of Harpin and his rapid ride to defend Lunete have been already discussed.

The adventure of Noire Espine contains a description of
night in the forest already referred to as the single occurrence of emotional implications attached to "nuit," but this
also emphasizes the necessity to find shelter -- not just
because night had fallen, but because it was extremely damp
in the forest and the damsel clearly needed a place to change
her clothing. The castle at which she shelters is the one
recently besieged by Harpin and she had news of the knight for
whom she is searching, so again the logic of the events com-
pels her to get up "quant vint que l'aube fu crevee" (4923).

Having found Yvain, the damsel reaches the castle of
Pesme Aventure with her two companions when "li jorz aloit
declinant" (5105). They are well entertained -- "la nuit fu
serviz au mangier / de tanz mes" and "la nuit totes enors li
firent" (5432; 5436) -- but "nuit" clearly means 'evening'
here. Yvain is in a hurry to reach court since we know the
younger daughter of Noire Espine has a time-limit to find a
champion, so again this is stressed by the hero arising
"isnelemant" (5446) "au main" (5442). Their haste is frustrated,
however, by the challenge given them after Mass; this Chrétien
defeats our expectation of a rapid journey to court and increases tension.

The departure from Pesme Aventure and arrival at Noire
Espine is not linked to the daily cycle although we are told
the journey takes "trestoz les jorz de la semainne" (5807),
and after a night's rest they leave for the court "l'andermain"

(5835). There is only one day left of the alloted time and
"fors del chastel cele nuit jurent" (5857) -- again, as so
frequently is the case, "nuit" has duration and does not refer
to 'nightfall'.

Haste is emphasized as Yvain leaves his lodging "a grant
besoing, / a l'aube aparissant" (5862-63), and hides until
"li jorz fu biax et granz" (5865). The hour of decision approaches, "jusqu'a po sera none basse, / et li derriens jorz
iert hui" (5884-85), as the wicked sister says. The duel
begins and lasts until dusk: "Li jorz vers la nuit se tret ...
la nuit qui vient oscure ... la nuiz aproche" (6199; 6214;
6229). The duel ends, the lawsuit is settled, and Yvain is
free to try to regain his lady's love. This he achieves
without further reference to the lapse of time since his goal
is no longer related to it.

The patterns of time in Yvain cannot be related in any
simple way to the interleaved pattern of the narrative --
references to the time of day are either causal or are logically important for the movement of the plot and the manner in
which Chrétien stresses the expectations of the reader. The
use of "demain" is related to this same concern of the author's
-- this word, with its implication of what is to come rather
than with what is, is concentrated almost exclusively in a few
key scenes. The first is the dialogue in which Lunete praises
Yvain and urges Laudine to meet him. Laudine: "Veigne enuit
ou demain" (1825). "That's impossible," says Lunete, "but I
have a messenger who can reach the court 'au moins jusqu'a

demain au soir'" (1832), and Laudine replies that she wishes
the boy to return "demain au soir resoit ci" (1836).

The second scene is the one in which Lunete tells Yvain
of her imminent danger, leading to the tension-filled situation we have discussed. She tells him that if she can find
no champion "l'en demain ... m'arde ou pande" (3600) and that
it is Yvain's fault "por cui demain serai a tort" (2621).

Related to this scene is the one at the castle threatened by Harpin -- two dangers are awaited the next day, Yvain's
and that of the lord. The lord of the castle tells Yvain:
"Et demain ocirra les quatre" (3861), and "a demain puis ce
duel atendre" (3870). Yvain replies, trying to keep up the
lord's spirits: "Se eles se reconfortoient / jusqu'a demain"
(3983-84), and that "demain a midi ne soie / au plus grant
afeire por soir" (3990-91). Then the narrator comments that
they all slept "jusqu'a demain a l'enjornee" (4023).

The final example of this use of "demain" concerns the
damsel searching for Yvain to help the young lady of Noire
Espine. The lord of the castle tells her Yvain just killed
the giant (Harpin), that "demain porroiz veoir le cors" (4908)
and that "vos metrai an la voie / demain" (4916-17). Lunete
also gives her directions and says that she will find Yvain
very soon, "ainz hui que demain" (4996).

In Chrétien's Yvain, then, we can see a separation of
the pattern of time from the pattern of narrative. Time is
becoming independent of events, more objective though still
far from the mechanical inevitability to which we are

accustomed. There ia a definite change toward a more linear
concept with the idea of looking forward to events, the kind
of expectation which characterizes our future-oriented
society.

The structure of Sir Gawain and the Green Knight is
simpler than that of Yvain in two ways. First, the hero undertakes a single outward and return journey in search of a
definite objective, and secondly the poem is composed, like
the Roland, in a series of stanzas of inequal length.

There are, however, in addition, only two tests which
the hero has to undergo, a challenge to give and receive a
deadly blow, and a temptation to commit adultery. There is an
additional, though minor, probing of Gawain's integrity when
the guide taking him to the Green Chapel advises him to leave
by some other route (2091-2125).

This relative lack of complexity has been praised by a
recent editor of the poem:

> Gawain stands first among medieval English romances,
> and high among romances at large, in the strength
> of its plot. Even the greatest Arthurian stories,
> French no less than English -- such as Chrétien's
> Yvain or the prose Perlesvaus -- present strings
> of adventures, which, though sometimes system-
> atically 'interlaced', are often only loosely con-
> nected with each other and with the main theme.
> This discursive incoherence is apparently inher-
> ited from the older Celtic narratives from which
> so much of the Arthurian legend derives.[3]

This quotation, I suggest, reveals a not surprising
prejudice in favor of the literate tradition -- that Chrétien
is closer than is the author of Sir Gawain and the Green Knight

to an oral tradition, and his "discursive incoherence" may be characteristic rather of a non-literate culture (in spite of his own literacy), than of, by implication, tortuous Celtic thought processes. The answer to a question concerning the reason for the brevity and apparent disconnected structure of certain American Indian folktales was "it is because we know so much."[4] In an oral culture in which everything is held in memory the significance of many details -- and even the details themselves -- is tacitly understood. A literate man, with his poor memory which relies on the printed word, is only able to deal with relatively simple linear narratives, with strong unified plots.

Davis suggests that Sir Gawain and the Green Knight can be neatly divided according to the hero's two adventures, the central part being occupied by the attempted seduction preceded by the Green Knight's challenge and succeeded by Gawain's response. This pattern seems to be accepted by the scribe of the only existing manuscript who gave "the initial letters of lines 491, 1136, and 1998 ... prominence by long horizontal flourishes which extend right across the page, taking up the space ruled for a line of writing and so making a clear break in the sequence of the lines. These breaks came at points in the text at which the sense calls for a substantial pause."[5] Since Madden's edition (1839) these divisions have become accepted so that the poem is usually printed in four Fitts. Davis, then, suggests that the challenge occupies Fitt I, the temptation Fitts II and III, and Gawain's response Fitt IV.

Although I accepted the four-fold division, Davis seems to oversimplify, perhaps in his concern for symmetry. Fitt II begins with a charming description of the changing seasons, followed by Gawain's preparations for his journey. The hero reaches Sir Bertilak's castle about line 760, is challenged to exchange winnings about line 1100, and then retires to bed. The temptation by the lady of the castle does not begin before line 1190, after Sir Bertilak has left the castle to go hunting at the beginning of Fitt III (1126).

As well as these three large initials, "there are also five smaller coloured (sic) initials, extending over three lines with simpler ornament ... at lines 619 [beginning the description of Gawain's shield]; 763 [Gawain's approach to Bertilak's castle]; 1421 [the boar hunt]; 1893 [the last part of the fox hunt]; and 2259 [the return blow at the Green Chapel]."[6] Davis goes on to say that although these smaller capitals mark important points in the story, there are other equally significant stages which are not indicated.

The four main narrative divisions of Sir Gawain and the Green Knight are also temporal divisions, but the time indicators are not precise. Fitt I ends with a continuation of the season's festivities until "þat day ... til worþed an ende" (485), but Fitt II begins with a brief recapitulation and comment on Gawain's situation ("but þaȝ þe ende be heuy ȝe no wonder" [496]) before the description of the sequence of the seasons. The end of Fitt II is more precise; the company retires to bed: "Vche burne to his bed watz broȝt at þe laste, ful softe" (1120-21), and Fitt III begins early next

day: "Ful erly bifore þe day þe folk vprysen" (1126). Fitt

III similarly ends with the hero going to bed but the poet does

not break off clearly, but whets our appetites for more:

> Let hym ly3e þere stille,
>
> He hatz nere þat he so3t;
>
> And 3e wyl a whyle be stylle
>
> I schal telle you how þat wro3t.

> (1994-97)

The opening of Fitt IV also emphasizes Gawain's sleeplessness;

there is a description of the bitter night-time weather and

a picture of Gawain trying to rest but not sleeping:

> Þe leude lystened ful wel þat le3 in his bedde,
>
> Þa he lowkez his liddez, ful lyttel he slepes

> (2006-07)

From these remarks we may see that in <u>Sir Gawain and the

Green Knight</u> the relation of action to the day-night cycle is

certainly much less close than it is in the <u>Roland</u>, in which

action begins and ends as day begins and ends. We shall con-

sider these narrative breaks again later, particularly with

reference to the patterns of time.

Having accepted the four main divisions of the poem, can

we make any further divisions, perhaps using the stanzas as a

basis? The individual lines of the stanzas are not connected

one to the next by assonance as are those of the <u>Roland</u>. Each

line is a metrical unit -- the alliterative line characteristic

of Old English poetry -- but the lines are not units of

meaning as they are in the <u>Roland</u>. The style is hypotactic
with much use of conjunctions, and a sentence may continue
over several lines:

> 'Bi Mary,' quoþ þe menskul, 'me þynk hit an oþer;
> For were I worth al þe wone of wymmen alyue,
> And al þe wele of þe worlde were in my honde,
> And I shulde chepen and chose to cheue me a lorde,
> For þe costes þat I haf knowen vpon þe, kny3t, here
> Of bewte and debonerte and blyþe semblaunt,
> And þat I haf er herkkened and halde hit here trwee,
> Þer schulde no freke vpon folde bifore yow be chosen.
>
> (1269-75)

This is not a particularly unusual example.

Occasionally a sentence begun in one stanza continues
with the next:

> Wyth chynne and cheke ful swete,
> Boþe quit and red in blande,
> Ful lufly con ho lete
> Wyth lyppez smal la3ande.
> 'God moroun, Sir Gawayn,' sayde þat gay lady,
> '3e ar a sleper vnsly3e, þat mon mat slyde hider'
>
> (1204-07)

Frequently an action begun in one stanza will not be completed
until the next (the breaking up of the deer):

> Bi þe by3t al of þe þy3es
> Þe lappez þay lance bihynde;
> To hewe hit in two þay hy3es,

Bi þe bakbon to vnbynde.

Boþe þe hede and þe hals þay hwen of þenne,

And syþen sunder þay þe sydez swyft from þe chyne,

And þe corbeles fee þay kest in a greue

(1349-55)

Within the four major parts of the poem we must look to

larger divisions than merely stanzaic ones, then, and see if

these are related to any temporal patterns.

As we have done with other texts, let us see if the

journeys function in any way to separate blocks of action; we

saw how this was not possible in Yvain, but perhaps the more

straightforward arrangement of Sir Gawain and the Green Knight

will be different.

Davis again reveals his bias in regard to Gawain's journeys:

"Though the hero's two long journeys give obvious openings for

many [adventures], the author resisted the temptation" (xiv).[7]

This implies that Gawain's journeys are uneventful, but nothing

could be further from the truth. The adventures are, however,

described extremely briefly. On the journey out:

At vche warþe oþer water þer þe wy3e passed

He fonde a foo hym byfore, bot ferly hit were,

And þat so foule and so felle þat fe3t hym byhode.

So mony meruayl bi mount þer þe mon fyndez.

Hit were to tore for to telle of þe tenþe dole.

Sumwhyle wyth wormez he werrez, and with wolues als,

Sumwhyle wyth wodwos, þat woned in þe knarrez,

Boþe wyth bullez and berez, and borez oþerquyle,

And etaynez, þat hym aneled of þe heȝe felle.

(715-23)

The return is equally full of incident:

Wylde wayez in þe worlde Wowen now rydez

On Gryngolet ...

Ofte he herbered in house and ofte al þeroute,

And mony aventure in vale, and venquyst ofte,

Þat I ne tyȝt at þis tyme in tale to remene.

(2479-83)

Gawain, in fact, encounters more and a wider variety of difficulties than Yvain: enemies at every crossing, dragons as
well as the more usual wild animals, giants and wild men of
the forest, and, unlike Yvain, he is not always able to find
a convenient castle in which to spend the night. Sometimes
"ner slayn wyth þe slete he sleped in his yrnes / Mo nyȝtez
þen innoghe in naked rokkez" (729-30).

Gawain's journeys, then, are qualitatively different from
the journeys in earlier texts such as the Roland, but only
quantitatively different from those in Yvain. In Yvain, the
journeys are an essential part of the plot and the adventures
a necessary part of the hero's moral progress. In Sir Gawain
and the Green Knight, the emphasis has shifted, concentrating
on a definite goal for Gawain's outward journey, which is
therefore a quest, but the adventures which I suggest are part
of the traditional structure of romance have not been completely
eliminated. There is a great difference of stress between that
accorded the major events of the poem, the challenge and

response which occupy most of it, and that given the briefly summarized events of Gawain's journeys. In Yvain we were unable to use the journeys as elements which mark boundaries between major acts or scenes (as we could do in the earlier poems we have considered); in Sir Gawain and the Green Knight we shall attempt to do this but must keep in mind that the journeys are part of the essentially linear continuous sequence of events and contain information and description which may be significant.

The initial challenge of the Green Knight is for Gawain to give a blow and to receive one a year later. Gawain's outward journey is in direct response to this and of course is related to the time-limit set. But since the Green Knight gave no address, Gawain has to allow adequate time to find his mysterious challenger. He begins to concern himself with his journey at the end of September and finally leaves Camelot on November 2nd, as we have seen. This attitude toward time is of course quite different from that in the Roland, and also different from that of Chrétien, who appears to allow a vague three days for Yvain to find a geographically very indefinite magic fountain. But Gawain's two months seem not unreasonable from a modern point of view, and in fact he has, it turns out, almost a week in hand since he arrives at Bertilak's castle on December 24th.

Gawain's successful quest for the Green Knight's abode includes an interlude of six or seven days during which he undergoes his second test, concealed by his host in the sug-

gestion of an exchange of winnings. He then <u>continues</u> his
journey to the Green Chapel, completes the beheading challenge,
and returns to the King's court.

The more carefully one examines <u>Sir</u> <u>Gawain</u> <u>and</u> <u>the</u> <u>Green</u>
<u>Knight</u>, the more difficult it becomes to find a neat symmetrical
structure and the closer the poem appears related to earlier
romances. Gawain's journey to the Green Chapel is interrupted many times although only two adventures are described
in detail, the first being his temptation at Bertilak's
castle and the second the attempt by the guide to dissuade
him from meeting the Green Knight. His quest is not complete
until after the beginning of Fitt IV:

> Þenne he boȝez to þe berȝe, aboute hit he walkez,
> Debatande with hymself quat hit be myȝt ...
> > 'We! Lorde,' quoþ þe gentyle knyȝt.
> > 'Wheþer þis be þe grene chapell?'

> > > (2178-79; 2185-86)

And insofar as the quest is one concerning self-knowledge, it
is not finished until Gawain recognizes his fault.

> Þat oþer stif mon in study stod a gret whyle,
> So agreued for greme he gryed withinne;
> Alle þe blode of his brest blende in his face,
> Þat al he schrank for schome þat þe schalk talked.

> > (2369-72)

Since a close look at Gawain's journeys tends to compli-
cate rather than to simplify the structure of the poem, let
us turn to the traditional manuscript divisions and see what

their relationship to elements of time (which we have already
briefly mentioned) can tell us about the attitudes of the poet
toward time.

The poem begins with a recapitulation of (mythic) British
history, setting the story in the golden age of King Arthur:
"Þe hendest, as I haf herde telle" (26). The place is Camelot
and the season Christmas -- it is, in fact, New Year's Day
when the adventure begins. The Green Knight enters, the challenge is issued and accepted, the visitor departs, and the
rest of the day is spent in feasting:

> Wyth alle maner of mete and mynstralcie boþe,
>
> Wyth wele walt þay þat day, til worþed an ende
>
> in londe.
>
> (484-86)

No time limit is mentioned.

Fitt II, like Fitt I, begins with a description which
embodies an idea of 'historical' linear time, including the
line "A ȝere ȝernes ful ȝerne, and ȝeldez neuer lyke" (498),
but then continues with a description of the cycle of the
seasons. The universal, however, becomes the particular, the
cyclic becomes linear, since we are brought to a particular
date, Michaelmas, and it is the particular Michaelmas at which
Gawain begins to think of his "anious uyage" (535). In a
sophisticated way, then, the poet contrasts and connects "cyclic
time or the time of nature [with] linear time or the time of
history."[8]

After Gawain's journey to the north and his welcome at

Bertilak's castle, the exchange of winnings agreement is made, and the people of the castle prepare for bed. At this point an attitude toward time which we have not previously encountered is demonstrated. This is implied by the use of artificial light:

> With mony leude ful ly3t and lemande torches
> Vche burne to his bed watz bro3t at þe laste,
> > ful softe.

> > > (1119-21)

Of course I do not imply that artificial light was not <u>used</u> before, but what is evident from the frequent occurrence of this and related incidents in <u>Sir</u> <u>Gawain</u> <u>and</u> <u>the</u> <u>Green</u> <u>Knight</u> is that the idea of independence from the natural cycle is becoming part of the cultural background. It is during the fourteenth century that the striking clock began to be seen on public buildings and the minute and second were invented, so that a day of twenty-four fixed and equal hours develops. Canonical hours based on twelve hours of light and twelve of darkness were no longer the only measure of daily time.[9]

Fitt III begins "ful erly bifore þe day þe folk vprysen" (1126) and Bertilak is out "bi þat any dayly3t lemed vpon erþe" (1137). This activity out-of-door is contrasted with the inactivity and tardiness indoors: "And Gawayn þe god mon in gay bed lyges, / Lurkkez quyl þe dayly3t lemed on þe wowes" (1179-80). This contrast continues through these scenes, in which the lady tries to seduce Gawain: outside is the natural active world tied to seasonal activities limited by the cycle

of light and darkness, while inside is the leisurely world of
words, artificially illuminated and thus free from the con-
straints of nature.

Bertilak's hunting is limited by the short winter days
-- he "drof þat day wyth joy / Thus to þe derk nyȝt" (1176-77),
and "he þer slowe bi þat þe sunne heldet" (1321), while Gawain
and the lady "made myry al day, til þe mone rysed" (1313),
that is, presumably till after sunset.

The next day Bertilak again is out before dawn:

> Bi þat þe coke hade crowen and cakled bot þryse,
> Þe lorde watz lopen of his bedde...er any day sprenged
>)1412-15)

but again is limited by the lack of daylight. He is "suande
þis wylde swyn til þe sunne schafted" (1467). On his return
he exchanges winnings with Gawain and they dine in the "clere
lyȝt of [waxen] torches" (1649-50).

On the third day Bertilak "ful erly ... watz diȝt" (1689)
and is in the field already before "vpon rak rises þe sunne"
(1695), while as for Gawain, "þe hende knyȝt at home slepes /
Withinne þe comly cortynes, on þe colde morne" (1731-32).
Bertilak, having killed the fox, returns home "for hit watz
neiȝ nyȝt" (1922), and he and Gawain exchange their winnings
for the third time. After farewells have been said, Gawain
"with ledes and lyȝt he watz ladde to his chambre" (1989).
The last night Gawain spends in the castle passes slowly,
filled only with his thoughts, since he is unable to sleep.
"Þe leude lystened ful wel þat leȝ in his bedde, / Þaz he

lowkez his leddez, ful lyttel he slepes; / Bi vch kok þat crue
he knwe wel þe steuen" (2006-08). He arises "er þe day
sprenged" (2009) and we are told that he is able to do this
because "þere watz ly3t of a lampe þat lemed in his chambre"
(2010). He travels some distance before "hit watz sone sesoun
þat þe sunne ryses þat tyde" (2085-86). This night crosses
the divisions between the end of Fitt III and the beginning
of Fitt IV, although the last lines of Fitt III concern Gawain
going to bed and the first of Fitt IV describe the wild night-
time weather and the hero's sleeplessness. The poet encourages
expectation in the reader, however, at the very end of Fitt
III:

> And 3e wyl a whyle be stylle
> I schal telle yow how þat wro3t.
>
> (1996-97)

We are kept, so to speak, on the edge of our seats. It seems
as if we are not expected to know the outcome of the story
beforehand. Even if this is only a convention, the implications
are of a different attitude than we saw, for example, in the
Roland.

The careful dissociation of the beginning and ending of
activity from the cycle of light and dark, which is so strongly
emphasized in Fitt III, seems to me to mark a very important
step in the direction of the development of an objective sense
of time. We shall now examine the use of individual words
related to time to see if we can find confirmation of this
development.

Of the twenty-nine occurrences of the word 'day' in Sir
Gawain and the Green Knight, almost half indicate a point in
time, a particular day, e.g., 'on þis day,' 'Nw 3eres day,'
'sayn Jonez day,' and so on. The remaining examples are
divided equally between the meaning of daylight (e.g., 'er
day sprenged'), greeting ('goud day'), and duration ('þer
dayes,' 'al day'). There is no reference to the quality or
brightness of the day, no direct association with action, as
we have seen, nor stress on repetitious sameness -- the contrary, in fact, since the great majority of occurrences
identify this or that day as different from others. As with
Yvain, almost two-thirds of the occurrences of 'day' are connected to the passage of time.

'Night' or its equivalents is used ten times, referring
to nightfall ('hit watz nie nyt'). Darkness is mentioned
directly but apart from this there are no qualitative connections. Although Bertilak is able to leave the castle
before daybreak, however, he is compelled by the onset of
darkness to begin his journey homeward, as we have seen.

'Morn' and 'morning' refer both to the following day
and to early in the day, frequently both meanings are implied:
'on þe morne' may have an adjective such as 'colde' or 'gray'
added, but the usual implication emphasizes the action to
come, as with 'demain' in Yvain.

Other parts of the day are referred to occasionally:
these are references to the canonical hours of "matynes" (755),
"euensong" (932), presumably at vespers, and "pryme" (1675).

"Mydmorn" (1073 and 1280), "myd-ouer-vnder" (1730), and "messe-
quyle" (1097) may also refer to canonical hours -- 'tierce,'
'none,' and 'prime' respectively.

The words 'tyme' and 'tyde' are surprisingly frequent,
with twenty-two and six occurrences respectively. Their
meanings are almost interchangeable, referring to a particular
occasion or a season, a longer period of time. 'At þis (þat)
tyme (tyde)' occurs twenty-three times with one or another of
these meanings. The words function objectively with few exceptions (e.g., "þe hy3e tyde" [932]) and seem to add to the
objective aspect of time.

But perhaps the most interesting reference to time in
the whole poem, as far as our investigation is concerned,
comes in the scene in which Gawain and the Green Knight have
their second meeting. The original challenge was for Gawain
to seek out this mysterious adversary and to meet him in a
year and a day, which he manages to do. The Green Knight first
welcomes Gawain and then praises him for his punctuality, for
being, precisely, 'on time':

> Iwysse þou art welcom, wy3e, to my place
>
> And þou hatz tymed þi trauayl as truee mon schulde
>
> (2441-42)

In Yvain, the hero was blamed first for breaking his promise
and then for being late; here Gawain is first praised for his
punctuality and then for keeping his word.

I should like to end consideration of Sir Gawain and the
Green Knight here by concluding that the relation between the

patterns of narrative and of time has become less obvious --
the concept of time is more objective, removed both from the
cycle of nature and the acts of men. We have moved into a
period in which being 'on time' is an important virtue.

The organization of Icelandic sagas has been the subject
of considerable discussion in recent years, ranging from attempts to redefine the various genres[10] to analyses of the
structure of groups of sags[11] or individual texts, using a
variety of approaches.

In his book on Njáls Saga, Lönnroth discusses the composi-
tional units of a saga, referring to suggestions of both Allen
and Clover. I shall apply some of these same ideas to Gunnlaugs
Saga and relate them to the patterns of time in this saga, but
first I wish to discuss the chapters into which Gunnlaugs Saga,
like the other sagas, was divided by early editors.

As Lönnroth says, "The chapter as a unit is clearly of
foreign origin.... Chapter divisions are notoriously incon-
sistent in many manuscripts.... The divisions -- indicated
in the medieval fashion by a large initial and/or rubric --
serve more as a table of contents than as a guide to structure"
(Njála MSS, p. 53). The Fornrit edition of Gunnlaugs Saga is
based on texts contained in two manuscripts, one of which
(Arne Magnæan, 557, 4to) is by far the more important and
contains approximately the first five-sixths of the narrative
as it is edited.[13]

I undertook an examination of a facsimile of this manuscript to see how the chapters of the edition are related to the large initials of the manuscript. In fact, the manuscript contains no initials, but a space has been left for them and occasionally the letter to be written is indicated, in normal size, beside the empty space. The manuscript breaks off at almost the end of chapter eleven of the edition.

There are eleven spaces left for large initials in the manuscript, and the corresponding part of the edition has eleven chapter beginnings, but there is not an exact agreement between the two systems. The following table sets out the situation. The phrases are given, including any letters which are inferred from the manuscript.

EDITION CHAPTER	EDITION PHRASE	MS SPACING OR PHRASE (if different)
I	Þorstéinn hét maðr	
II	Eitt sumar	NO SPACE
III	Um sumarit	
IV	Þenna tíma bjó...Illugi	(...sagt at) þenna tíma
V	Ǫnundr hét maðr	NO SPACE
		Ok þessu nær urði þau tíðendi (EXTRA INITIAL SPACE)
VI	Þenna tíma réð fyrir Nóregi	
VII	Þá réð fyrir Englandi	
VIII	Síðan siglir Gunnlaugr	
IX	Þenna tíma réð fyrir Svíþjóð	NO SPACE
X	Nú er at segja frá Gunnlaugi	
		Þer tóku land norðr (EXTRA INITIAL SPACE)
XI	Nú er at segja frá Hrafn	

In spite of the fact that these divisions do not all correspond, the phrases which introduce each new section have something in common -- they belong to a group of stock narrative phrases which Lönnroth calls "formulas." Lönnroth mentions motifs which may be introduced by these formulas, "such as a ride to the Althing or the introduction of characters," and says they may also serve as transitions "to call our attention to scene shifts." Among the examples he gives are "Nú er at segja frá X," "Nú," and "Síðan" (Njála MSS, p. 45).

Clover (p. 58ff), to whom Lönnroth refers, discusses the composition of sagas in terms of scenes. She recognizes that sagas are episodic in nature, that "the story is advanced in a series of relatively independent units following each other in paratactic sequence." She quotes, with approval, W. P. Ker's image of "a series of pictures rising in the mind, succeeding, displacing, and correcting one another,"[14] and mentions several other scholars, among them Andersson and Allen, who use this terminology. "Saga prose is a narrative of parataxis, consisting of 'verbal blocks loosely juxtaposed.'[15] In the purest form of scenic narration, these 'verbal blocks' are tripartite scenes ... without connecting narrative of any kind" (Clover, p. 64). It will not have escaped the reader's notice that the relation of paratactic construction to a series of pictures is precisely that which we discussed in our analysis of the Roland.

> Framing the dramatic center [of the saga scene] are
> the preface and the conclusion. In the preface,
> the scene is set and the conditions for the en-
> suing action are laid down. Persons, time, place,

and situation are named. The opening lines of
the scene fill or assist in this function, and
they tend to be of a few standard types. Maðr
het or Maðr er nefndr are common scene openers.
The most usual way of opening a scene is to
announce time [emphasis added], and it is significant that most of the saga formulas are
those which announce time-occasion. They may
be specific: Þá um sumarit, um haustit var þat,
etc. Other times they indicate relative time:
littlu síðar, nokkurn síðar, í þenna tíma, etc.
Other time-phrases ... draw the narrative from
the historical-general to the particular time-
point of a single event: Þat var einn hvern
dag, etc. Sometimes time-phrases refer to the
narrator's time, the time of the telling, rather
than the time of the story events: ... Nú er
at segja frá, etc.
(Clover, p. 62)

Clover goes on to discuss the conclusions of the "scenes" which

tend to be

> of a few standard types. Often scenes end on a
> note of time passing ... [or] one strand of the
> story [may be left] in a state of continued
> action while taking up another strand [but] the
> most common device by which scenes are closed
> is the departure of the participants.
> (Clover, pp. 62-63)

The preceding quotations clearly suggest that saga prose has

many of the structural characteristics of the earlier medieval

narratives which have already been analyzed, even though the

form of those narratives (the Roland, for example) is verse

and not prose. Clover also implies a connection between time

patterns and narrative patterns, and also mentions journeys as

"the most common device" for ending a scene.

The breaks in Gunnlaugs Saga, whether in the manuscript

or in the printed edition, are indicated by those kinds of

formulas which Clover and Lönnroth refer to as marking changes

of scene in their discussions of saga narrative elements: of

the thirteen breaks, three refer to historical time (that is,
to the rulers of Norway, Rngland, and Sweden), one to a
historical event (Christianization), one to the life-time of
a historical figure (Illugi Halkelsson), one to a specific
summer, one to an unspecified summer, and one to relative
time ("Siðan"). Two refer to the time of the narrative ("Nú
er at segja frá ...), and two use the formula "X hét maðr."
The only large initial space or chapter heading which does
not fit these formulas is the space at "Þer tóku land norðu"
which marks an important point in the story -- Gunnlaug's return to Iceland just before Helga's wedding to Hrafn -- but
in fact this does indicate the opening of a preface to a
"scene." The scenes which are indicated by initial spaces in
the manuscript and by chapter headings in the edition, however,
are not only "scenes" in the narrative. We shall examine how
these scenes are linked, having first referred briefly to other
ways of diving Gunnlaugs Saga into larger narrative elements.

Andersson's six-part thematic division of sagas (Introduction : conflict : climax : revenge : reconciliation : after-
math) does not seem particularly useful for the problems I am
concerned with, and he himself says that "there are several
peculiarities in the structure of Gunnlaugs Saga.... After [a]
lengthy prelude the conflict is disproportionately brief....
The revenge is even more simplified [and] there is no official
reconciliation" (Andersson, 1967, pp. 127-28).

The chapter divisions in Gwyn Jones' translation[16] can
be organized into five major 'Acts', but this is more a matter

of editorial discretion than something innate in the text.

I		Introduction to the three main characters
	(i)	Introduction to Helga
	(ii)	Introduction to Gunnlaug (this includes the meeting of Gunnlaug and Helga)
	(iii)	Introduction to Hrafn (but this includes a good deal of Gunnlaug's character development)
II		Development of Conflict
	(i)	Gunnlaug's character development (continued)
	(ii)	Hrafn's character development
	(iii)	Gullnaug's wishes frustrated
III		The Challenge
IV		The Challenge Completed
V		Consequences

I am not concerned, at this moment, with attempting to redefine genre in Icelandic literature, or to make any general
statements about sagas, but Clover's categories seem to be
useful in my study of Gunnlaugs Saga. I shall combine her
idea of "scene" with the approach of considering journeys as
narrative dividers which I have previously used, and try to
see what connections these have to patterns of time in the
saga. It must be noted here that because of the long time-
span of the narrative (from the birth of Helga to the death of
Gunnlaug would logically be about twenty-five years), the story
moves at a leisurely pace. The basic time-unit is the cycle
of the year rather than that of the day -- spring or summer
take the place of sunrise, and autumn takes the place of night-

fall. At significant moments in the text, however, actions
are linked to the daily cycle; Gunnlaug's departure to Borg
from his father's house, his final arrival at Gilsbakki when
he comes back to Iceland, and the pursuit of Hrafn before the
final duel, for example. Local journeys are often linked to
the daily cycle, but voyages to the cycle of seasons.

The long opening scene is prefaced by a genealogy which
places Thorstein geographically and socially. The preface to
the first scene continues with an imprecise seasonal reference, 'one summer,' and the inward journey of Bergfinn the
Norwegian. Thorsteinn meets him, invites him to stay, and the
winters passes. The temporal focus becomes sharper with the
preface to the next journey -- 'one day in spring' -- and a
more specific journey, that of both men to repair Thorstein's
booth. It is a hot day, and the drama develops: Thorstein has
a dream and the Norwegian interprets the dream. The men dis-
agree, return home in the evening, and the Norwegian departs
in the summer, "ok er hann nú ór sǫgunni" ('and he is now out
of the saga' [55]). This is a good example of a scene which
contains several important elements. The scene begins with
a time-reference and a specific journey and ends with a time-
reference and a journey. The dramatic element is significant
and involves considerable dialogue.

The saga can be divided similarly into about fifty
scenes of which a few more will be briefly described, the next
one being marked by the space left for an initial:

Preface	'In the summer' ("um sumarit" [55]) Thorstein gets ready to go to the Althing
Drama	He orders Jofrid to expose the child she is carrying
Conclusion	Thorstein rides to the Althing
	Jofrid gives birth to a fine girl 'later' (This seems a poor preface)
Drama	Jofrid arranges for the child's fostering by Olaf's family
Conclusion	The servant leaves the country; "ok er hann nú ór sǫgunni" (57)
Preface	Thorstein comes home
Drama	Jofrid tells him the child was exposed
Conclusion	Six years pass without the truth being known
Preface	Thorstein rides to Olaf's
Drama	Helga is identified as his child
Conclusion	The family rides home, and Helga is brought up with much love

This group of scenes obviously belongs together in some kind
of unit ("Introduction to Helga"), but each scene is equally
clearly distinct from the preceding and following one; a
journey often separates the scenes although not in every case
is there a formulaic opening and closing. The time period
covered is about six years.

The next section ("Introduction to Gunnlaug") begins with
an 'initial space' and an opening formula, "Þenna tíma bjó
uppi á ... Gilsbakka " ('At that time there was living, at
Gilsbakki' [58]), but is much shorter than the previous section.
After the preliminary genealogy and physical and psychological

description of the hero, we are told that at twelve years old
he wished to go abroad but his father opposed his wishes --
a short scene which itself is a preface to a more detailed
examination of the same conflict. The latter begins "ok
einnhvern morgin var þat, allitlu síðan ..." ('and on a certain
morning, a little later' [59]), continues with a dialogue of
conflict between father and son, and ends with Gunnlaug riding
away to Thorstein's place. The first two sections are brought
together here since Helga and Gunnlaug meet and become friends.
The final scene begins "ok einnhvern dag, er menn sátu í stofu
at Borg" ('and on a certain day when people were sitting in
the living room at Borg' [60]), continues to describe the
mock-betrothal, and the section concludes with everyone
thinking it very amusing.

Hrafn is introduced in the next section (not indicated
by an initial space), which begins "Ǫnundr hét maðr, er bjó
suðr at Mosfelli" ('There was a man called Ǫnundr who lived
south at Mosfell' [61]). Historical time is indicated by a
reference to the Christianization of Iceland (1000 AD) and to
the period in which Skapti was Lawspeaker (1004-1030) -- not
a precise match but close enough to be covered by the phrase
"ok þessir men, er nú eru nefndir, váru allir uppi á einn
tima ('and all these men who have just been named were all
living at the same time' [62]; emphasis added). In this same
long preface is another time-reference: six years have passed
and Gunnlaug is now eighteen. The drama, an argument with a
farmer in which Gunnlaug utters his first verse in the saga,

is again preceded and concluded by a journey. The exposition
of Gunnlaug's character begins.

The three leisurely introductory sections have proceeded
in a similar manner. The social, temporal and geographical
settings are given in rather general terms, then the focus
narrows to a particular time and place and to one or two in-
dividuals. The correlation between scene, journey, and time
indication is frequent but not absolute.

The tempo of the narrative speeds up, the scenes become
more sharply delineated as Gunnlaug sets out like the hero of
a romance to achieve a reputation so that he can win his bride.
Thorsteinn says, "Gunnlaug skal fara útan ok skapa sik eptir
góðra manna siðum" ('Gunnlaug shall journey abroad and model
himself after good men' [68]). First he plans to go abroad,
then his journey is partly frustrated by his desire for Helga,
and finally the agreement is made to a betrothal limited in
time.

Gunnlaug makes journeys to Norway, England, Dublin, the
Orkneys, Gautland, and Sweden. Each visit is a complete unit
prefaced and concluded by a journey and a seasonal reference
("um haustit"; "þenna vetr"; "um várit" and so on) and, of
course, a reference to the ruler of the place. In most cases
Gunnlaug arrives, has an interview with the ruler, receives
gifts (or in the case of Norway, makes an enemy!), and departs.
The visit to England, however, includes more than one scene:

Preface   Gunnlaug arrives

Drama   Presents a poem

Conclusion	The king rewards him and invites him to stay
Preface	'One morning early'
Drama	Conflict with berserk
Conclsion	Gunnlaug lends money
Preface	Gunnlaug meets the king 'a short time later'
Drama	Gunnlaug discusses the problem
Conclusion	Gunnlaug refuses to accept the situation
Preface	Again he meets the berserk 'a little later'
Drama	Challenge to duel
Conclusion	They part, to meet in three days
Preface	The king lends Gunnlaug a sword
Drama	The duel: Gunnlaug kills the berserk
Conclusion	Gunnlaug gains fame, plans to leave

These scenes do not begin and end with standard formulas, but all fit snugly together to form a longer scene which does so begin and conclude. Gunnlaug's following visits are much briefer, and each is composed in a single standard form: arrival, exchange of poem and gifts, departure.

A complete analysis shows that of the approximately fifty scenes about thirty are separated fron others by a journey. Those which are not, are themselves part of a longer section, like the one of Gunnlaug at Ethelred's court in London. A sequence of significant action may be expanded paratactically, sometimes with repetition, in a way similar to that of the laisses in the Roland. Gunnlaug's successive

visits to royal courts is an example of this, as is the
repetition of Hrafn's request for Helga's hand in marriage
at two successive meetings of the Althing. The final duel
between Gunnlaug and Hrafn is itself composed of perhaps five
small scenes, as a movie would break up the action into several successive 'shots':

Preface	'In the morning at sunrise they saw other'
Drama	Battle arrangements
Conclusion	Agreement
Preface	General battle
Drama	Poems tells sequence of deaths
Conclusion	All minor characters dead
Preface	Final duel begins
Drama	Dialogue after Hrafn wounded
Conclusion	Gunnlaug goes for water
Preface	Gunnlaug brings water
Drama	Hrafn wounds Gunnlaug: exchange of dialogue
Conclusion	Hrafn dies
Preface	Guides help Gunnlaug
Drama	Gunnlaug's final verses
Conclusion	Gunnlaug dies

Unlike the other texts we have considered, Gunnlaugs
Saga is prose, and yet has many of the characteristics of
early paratactic verse, such as that of the Roland. The
structure is discontinuous with scenes either succeeding each
other with little grammatical connection, or occasionally

linked in a group through the connections of a particular action. Scene change is frequently -- though not always -- indicated by a time phrase of the varying types that Clover mentions, but the pattern of time is certainly not linear. The first of the three introductory sections fills six years, then the second swoops back to describe Gunnlaug's family, and takes him up to his twelfth year. With Hrafn we are not given his age but merely told that "all these men" were flourishing at the same time. Hrafn's and Gunnlaug's travels are set out in linear time and match each other well, as we saw in the earlier chapter, but they are not described simultaneously. First we are told the adventures of one, then we swoop back again to catch up with the other: "Nú er at segja frá X."

The international voyages are connected to the seasons -- naturally enough, since spring or summer was the time to sail and autumn the time to make for home -- but there is not the straightforward kind of relationship between the natural cycle and action that we saw in the Roland. Similarly, men sometimes set out in the morning, reach their destination and return in the evening, but this seems to be convenient or by chance rather than by cultural necessity. The final pursuit of Hrafn by Gunnlaug uses the daily cycle, but for dramatic effect: "Gunnlaugr ... kom þar at kveldi jafnan, sem Hrafn hafði áðr verit um nóttina" ('Gunnlaug always arrived in the evening where Hrafn had been the night before" [100]).

It is difficult to say whether the structural and temporal

patterns are characteristic more of an oral or of a literary
text. Structurally the saga seems very close to oral tradition,
but the temporal pattern is less conclusive -- there are quasi-
historical references to events outside the narrative, for
example. The resemblance of the structural pattern to that
of the Roland is certainly remarkable. We can surely agree
that there is evidence for strong traditional influence. In
the next narrative, "The Shipman's Tale," we shall encounter
a sense that time is more objective and can be measured by a
mechanical device.

Chaucer's style is an extremely sophisticated and subtle
instrument, varied by him according to subject, speaker,
situation, and relationships, as Charles Muscatine[17] has shown.
In "The Shipman's Tale," as in other of Chaucer's fabliaux,[18]
the realistic details of the plot are complete -- nothing is
omitted which is necessary for a complete understanding of
the story. Regarding "The Miller's Tale," Muscatine remarks,
"We have a scrupulous accounting of days of the week and of
hours of the crucial day ... the great mass of ... detail
achieves an extraordinary solidity" (p. 224). "The Shipman's
Tale" is not as detailed as that of the Miller, but nothing
is left to chance nor anything superfluous added.

The humor of the story depends on the coordination of
the movements of the husband, the monk, and the wife, and the
accounting for an transfer of a sum of money which is first
borrowed from the husband by the monk, then given to the wife.

The husband asks the monk for it, is told that the wife has the money, but she refuses to part with it, saying she thought it was a gift.

The style is complex -- hypotactic, with frequent run-on lines:

> A wyf he hadde of excellent beautee;
> And compaignable and revelous was she,
> Which is a thyng that causeth more dispence
> Than worth is al the chiere and reverence
> That men hem doon at festes and at daunces.

(lines 3-7)

The introductory lines prepare us for the story with vague hints of what is likely to come. The reader is full of expectation, remembering, perhaps, that in the General Prologue to the Canterbury Tales the Shipman is described as being a deceitful character. We are told that the merchant was thought to be clever because he was rich; his expenses were great because "his wyf was fair" (22); the wife was "revelous" (4); and their frequent visitor, the young monk, was "a fair man and a bold" (25). Marital deceit seems likely.

The plot unfolds in a logical linear manner. After we are introduced to the characters, we are told the husband plans to leave town the next day. While the husband does his accounts in the early morning, the monk and his wife are in close conversation in the garden. Dinner is taken hastily when it is "passed pryme" (88) -- that is, past mid-morning -- and afterwards the monk borrows one hundred francs, and then goes home. Next morning, the husband leaves for Bruges, and the following Sunday the monk arrives, agrees to give the wife a hundred francs in exchange for sexual favors (already hinted at), and they spend the night together. Next morning the monk rides home. The husband returns home when his business is finished early to leave at once for Paris on further business. He meets the monk who tells him the hundred francs have already been paid back. When he return home again, he asks his wife about the debt and is told she thought the money was a gift.

What patterns of time and narrative can we find in this story? It is, in fact, difficult to find any repeated or regular patterning. There are several journeys involved but their relation to the rest of the narrative is not consistent. The monk's arrival is part of his regular travels, since we are told, he had "licence, / By cause he was a man of heigh prudence, / And eek an officer, out for to ride, / To seen hir graunges and hire bernes wyde, / And unto Seint-Denys he comth anon" (63-67). After the preliminary arrangement is made between the monk and the wife, the monk leaves, followed by the husband next day, and then the monk returns. But the husband's business trip is described in some detail:

> his prentys wel hym gydeth,
> Til he came into Brugges murily
> Now gooth this marchant faste and bisily
> Aboute his nede, and byeth and creaunceth.
>
> (299-303)

On his return home we are given his reasons for leaving again for Paris:

> For he was bounden in a reconyssaunce
>
> To paye twenty thousand sheeld anon.
>
> (330-21)

And we are told of his activities in Paris.

> [He] payd ... in Parys
>
> To certeyn Lumbardes, redy in hir hond,
>
> The somme of gold, and gat of him his bond;
>
> And hoom he gooth, murie as a papejay
>
> (366-69)

The monk's journeys, except for the first one, are given little
description and are often only part of a sentence -- the plot
is their justification: he "rideth to his abbeye" (298);
"ycomen is daun John" (308); or he "wente his way" (319).

The one scene which is repeated (the wife's sexual in-
tercourse, first with the monk, then with her husband) is
given significantly different treatment although similar
phrases describe the actual sex. With the monk, the financial
transaction takes place first:

> This faire wyf acorded with daun John
>
> That for thise hundred frankes he should al nyght
>
> Have hire in his armes bolt upright;
>
> And this acord parfourned was in dede.
>
> In myrthe al nyght a bisy lyf they lede
>
> Til it was day ...
>
> (314-19)

When the merchant returns from his business trip, his wife

meets him at the gate "And al that nyght in myrthe they bisette
... Whan is was day ... this marchant seyde ... 'I am a litel
wrooth / With you, my wyf" (375, 377, 382-83). Here, sex
takes precedence over the conversation about money, whereas with
the monk the reverse is true.

The structure in linear, then, with very little repetition even when this is obviously feasible, and the journeys
are integrated into the narrative. The pattern of time is
similarly irregular, in that there is no consistent reason
for time being mentioned except, of course, the necessity of
the plot which depends on timing.

The husband works in his counting-house "til it was passed
pryme" (88), while his wife and the monk converse until "it
was pryme of day" (206). The monk borrows money "at after-
dyner" (255) and then leaves some time later. The merchant
departs at some indeterminate time the next day, the monk
arrives the following Sunday and leaves sometime the next day.
The merchant's return journey home and then to Paris and home
again are nowhere connected to any time or season. In fact,
the only references to a specific time of day (apart from
"pryme" and "after-dyner") are to the morning after the two
bouts of sexual activity, "til it was day" and "when it was
day," quoted above. Similarly, "nyght" is used only for the
duration of this activity, again as already quoted.

There are no references to seasons, festivals, or, with
one exception, days of the week. The natural cycle of day and
night is only part of the action of the story in a quantitative

sense -- 'night' is a measure of duration and 'day' is a
point at which this particular activity ceases. There is,
then, no pattern of time any more than there is a consistent
pattern of narrative. The references to time are completely
dependent upon the requirements of the plot, rather than in
any sense the reverse. There is a strong sense of busy-ness,
of impatience, both in regard to the satisfaction of physical
desires (eating and sex), and in the mercantile activities
of the husband. This produces a feeling of time that passes
irrevocably, of chances that must not be missed, of a linear
sense of time. The fact that the monk measures the hour with
his pocket sundial ("by my chilyndre it is pryme of day" [206]),
and not by looking at the sun or hearing the monastery bell,
shows, I think, that Chaucer's society has removed itself
further from the time of Nature. The monk's rather ostentatious
gesture may imply that a "chilyndre" was something of a status
symbol, as an expensive watch is today. Similar instruments
were still in use in the Pyrenees in the ninteenth century.[19]

The texts we have discussed in this chapter show an interesting variety in their struture, both of narrative and of
time.

Gunnlaugs Saga is paratactic, episodic, and contains many
"formulaic" phrases which are frequently used at the beginning
and ending of a scene. This structural pattern is close to
that of the Roland. But the pattern of time is more linear,
and there are references to historical events outside the

sequence of events of the narrative.

The other texts are much more "literary" in their characteristics. Style is more complex and linear, giving rise to
expectation which the temporal sequence often emphasizes.
Time is less connected to action or linked to effect, and seems
to be becoming more objective and less qualitative. Particu-
larly in <u>Sir</u> <u>Gawain</u> <u>and</u> <u>the</u> <u>Green</u> <u>Knight</u> and in "The Shipman's
Tale" time is less a necessity than a convenient concept
around which a story can be constructed.

[1]Erich Auerbach, *Mimesis*, Chapter 6: "The Knight Sets Forth." A random example showing the run-on style and the sequence of subordinate clauses:

> Et ses enuiz tot ades croist
> que quan que il vit li angroist
> et quan que il ot li enuie;
> mis se voldroit estre a la fuie
> toz seus en si salvage terre
> que l'en ne le seüst ou querre,
> ne nus hom ne fame ne fust
> que de lui noveles seüst
> ne plus que s'il fust en abisme.
> (2783-91)

[2]Eugene Vinaver, *The Rise of Romance*, Chapter V: "The poetry of interlace."

[3]*Sir Gawain and the Green Knight*, (eds.) J. R. R. Tolkien and E. V. Gordon; 2nd ed., Norman Davis, p. xiv.

[4]Daniel F. Melia, Department of Rhetoric, University of California, Berkeley, personal communication.

[5]*Sir Gawain and the Green Knight*, p. xii.

[6]*Sir Gawain and the Green Knight*, p. xii.

[7]Perhaps we should be grateful that Homer was unable to resist a similar temptation in *The Odyssey*!

[8]Morton Bloomfield, "Sir Gawain and the Green Knight: An Appraisal."

[9]See above Chapter I, and Bertrand H. Bronson, "Concerning 'Houres Twelve," *Modern Language Notes*, 68 (December 1953), 515-21.

[10]Joseph Harris, "Genre and Narrative Structure in some Islendinga Þættir," *Scandinavian Studies*, 44 (1972), 1-27; Lars

Lönnroth, "The Concept of Genre in Saga Literature," Scandin-
avian Studies, 47 (1975), 419-26; Joseph Harris, "Genre in the
Saga Literature," Scandinavian Studies, 47 (1975), 427-36;
Theodore M Andersson, "Splitting the Saga,"   Scandinavian
Studies, 47 (1975), 437-41.

    [11]Theodore M. Andersson, The Icelandic Family Saga: An
Analytical Reading (Cambridge, Mass.: Harvard University Press,
1967).

    [12]Richard F. Allen, Fire and Iron: Critical Approaches
to Njáls Saga (Pittsburgh: University of Pittsburgh Press,
1971); Lars Lönnroth, Njáls Saga: A Critical Introduction
(Berkeley and Los Angeles: University of California Press,
1975); Lars Lönnroth, "Structural Divisions in the Njála
Manuscript," Arkiv för Nordisk Filologi, 90 (1975), 49-79;
Carol J. Clover, "Scene in Saga Composition," Arkiv för Nordisk
Filologi, 89 (1974), 57-83.

    [13]Corpus Codicum Islandicorum Medii Aevi, "The Arne
Magnæan Manuscript," 557, 4to (Copenhagen: Munksgaard, 1940),
p. 11.

    [14]W. P. Ker, Epic and Romance, p. 237.

    [15]Erich Auerbach, Mimesis, p. 102.

    [16]Erik the Red and Other Icelandic Sagas, selected and
translated with an introduction by Gwyn Jones (London: Oxford
University Press, 1961).

    [17]Charles Muscatine, Chaucer and the French Tradition
(Berkeley and Los Angeles: University of California Press,
1957).

[18]Since "The Shipman's Tale" is regarded as a fabliau, it would be interesting to compare Chaucer's version with an oral folktale analogue. But although the tale has been classified as Tale Type 1420 according to the Stith Thompson Types of the Folktale, only "one oral example [can be cited] ... and there is some question as to whether it should be in the Type Index at all" (Utley, p. 594). See Francis Lee Utley, "Some Implications of Chaucer's Folktales," Laographia (Athens: 1965), 588-99. See also W. F. Bryan and Germaine Dempster, Sources and Analogues of Chaucer's Canterbury Tales (New York: Humanities Press, 1958), 439-46; and J. W. Spargo, "Chaucer's 'Shipman's Tale'; The Lover's Gift Regained," Folklore Fellows' Communications, no. 91 (Helsinki, 1930). These discuss literary analogues only.

[19]See "Hoveden's Practica Chilindri" (ed. and tr.) E. Brock, Essays on Chaucer, II, iii (London: The Chaucer Society, 1874). The diagram in Hoveden represents an instrument identical to one in the Science Museum, London, F.A.B. Ward, Handbook of the Collections Illustrating Time Measurement (London: H. M. Stationary Office) 1955: Part II, p. 14 (text); 1947: Part I, plate III (illustration).

CONCLUSION

The aim of this investigation has been to try to develop
a new approach to the differences between oral and written
literature. Anthropological evidence indicates that the concepts of time are closely related to literacy and non-literacy,
which suggests that an examination of a variety of medieval
texts with regard to time might prove useful in refining the
differences between the two categories of literature.

Two particular aspects of time and their relation to
narrative have been considered. First, duration and the
question of chronology: does a particular event occupy an appropriate quantity of time, and does the narrative as a whole
take place within a continuous and logical time-frame? Second,
the problem of sequence is emphasized, and the relation of
time-sequence to the pattern of the suceession of events is
discussed. If regular patterns can be observed are they linear
or cyclic, or does the pattern of time, particularly in its
natural cycles, dominate the pattern of narrative or is the
sequence of events independent of such cycles?

The contrasts I have been looking for are between the
idea of exclusively cyclic time (which, it is suggested, is
characteristic of a non-literate culture), and that of linear
time which is by and large characteristic of a literate culture. I wished to discover whether these two different concepts are connected to related structural traits -- whether a
text with a cyclic concept of time has a cyclic narrative

style, whether it is paratactic, discontinuous and repetitive, and one in which duration is seen only in terms of events which fill a unit of time. A text with a linear time concept may be structurally linear, with more hypotaxis, being more con- tinuous and less repetitive; time may have duration outside the sequence of events. Since an oral text is part of a traditional shared culture, the story is likely to be known, and less emphasis is placed on expectation and more on the eleboration of "set pieces." With a story created by a literate author -- even out of traditional material -- the audience may well not know the outcome and the author can add to the audience's pleasure by withholding information or setting time-limits by which a task must be completed. As literacy and a sense of history develop, time is seen as more objective, quantitative, and less directly related to the natural world and the lives of men.[1]

The texts chosen were not selected in order to prove a point, but to cover a wide range of material with which I am familiar. The Song of Roland is accepted by many as an oral composition, while "The Shipman's Tale" and Yvain are of known literary authorship, and Sir Gawain and the Green Knight is certainly a literary creation. The other texts fall in the area between -- Beowulf particularly having passionate advo- cates on both side of the oral/literary fence.

This investigation gives a spectrum of results which confirms the ideas of the relation between literacy and time -- concepts put forward by anthropologists -- and reinforces

the idea of characteristically different structural patterns
of oral and literary texts which I synthesized from several
different sources.

To summarize, I shall begin by contrasting the two
opposite ends of the spectrum and then discuss those texts
which cannot so readily be classified.

The Song of Roland is a perfect example for illustrating
the ideas we have discussed. Structurally, it is paratactic,
discontinuous from the element of verse, to laisse, to group
of laisses, to "Acts." The style is appositional and the action
moves jerkily, held up by repetitions which serve to intensify
emotion. There is no expectation. With regard to time, there
is little 'realism' and a chronology of events is impossible
to construct since time, too, is discontinuous, being presented
in the cycle of day and night to which the events are closely
linked. The cycle of time either initiates or ends actions,
or is described in qualitative terms such as "beautiful" or
"evil."

For the three clearly literary works, we have an almost
completely opposite situation. Although Sir Gawain and the
Green Knight is composed in stanzas as in the Roland, the
style of the Middle English poem as well as its narrative
structure is much more hypotactic and linear, as are Yvain and
"The Shipman's Tale." In all three texts time forms a significant element in the plot and this, not repetition, is used
by the authors to produce emotion in the audience and the
characters. This is particularly true in Yvain where there

are several tense moments caused by this technique. A chronology of events can be constructed, either for almost the
whole narrative, or, in Yvain, for significant parts of it.
Time is adequately accounted for.

Times becomes successively more objective in these three
texts; in Yvain the action is still somewhat linked to "natural"
time, in Sir Gawain and the Green Knight there is a definite
conflict between the time of nature and the artificial time
of man, while in "the Shipman's Tale" time is specifically
ordered by man-made instruments.

Among the intermediate texts, Atlakviða is close to the
Roland. The narrative is broken up by journeys which are outside time, no chronology can be constructed, and the style
concentrates the audience's attention by repetition at key
points.

Gunnlaugs Saga is structurally close to the Roland in
that the style of the narrative -- even though it is prose --
is extremely paratactic. The crisis of the plot, however, like
that of the later texts, depends on a time-limit, and the
story is clearly connected to known historical events. There
is a sense of linear time, in that the Christian present of
the narrator is contrasted to the past when Iceland was heathen,
although there is also a strong sense of the recurring seasons.
The plot itself seems influenced by continental romance, in
which tender emotions are treated as of more importance than
is usual in a saga.

Most of the discussion concerning Beowulf's oral or

literary origin centers on the question of the poem's formulaic composition. It is a complicated issue, confused by technical questions of definitions, but is admirably discussed by Duggan (chapter two and p. 219). Using the approach of this dissertation, I should put Beowulf in the literary group. There is an extremely powerful feeling of linear time both within the poem itself and in the way the audience is distanced in time from the action by the narrator. As has already been pointed out, nearly all the "digressions" involve shifts in time, some of them relating historical events which are contrasted with the present time of the poem -- which is also the past for the audience. A chronology can be roughly constructed, but there is little sense of objective time.

Contrasting Beowulf with Gunnlaugs Saga, I should say that Beowulf is the product of a literate culture using traditional material, whereas Gunnlaugs Saga is the product of a non-literate culture using some literary material.

The following diagram sets out several of the polarities in this dissertation, but the reader must remember that the diagram represents relative positions and not absolute values, nor does it suggest any evolutionary trend from non-literate to literate. To simplify the diagram, not all texts are represented in all categories. It will be obvious that some polarities overlap others.

Legend for Diagrams

Am   - Atlamál

Legend for Diagrams (cont.)

At   - Atlakviða

B   - Beowulf

GK   - Sir Gawain and the Green Knight

GS   - Gunnlaugs Saga

ST   - The Shipman's Tale

Y   - Yvain

STRUCTURE AND STYLE

Paratactic	Discontinuous	Repetitive	No Expectation No Impatience
R	R	R	R
GS	GS		At
At	At	At	Am
Am	Am	Am	B
		GS	GS
B	B	B	ST
			GK
GK	GK	ST . GK . Y	Y
ST . Y	ST . Y		

| Hypotactic | Continuous | Non-repetitive | Expectation Impatience |

TIME

Cyclic	Chronology not possible	"Mythic" past	Cycle of Time linked to Action	No Punctuality	Subjective Qualitative
R	R	R	R	R	R
	At	At		At	
	Am	Am		Am	
		GK . Y			
B	B	B	B	B	B
GS	GS	GS	GS	GS	GS
Y	Y		Y	Y	Y
			GK	GK	GK
			ST	ST	ST
GK . ST	GK . ST				
Linear	Chronology possible	"Historic" past	Time Independent of Action	Punctuality	Objective Quantitative

←——————————→

My analysis of the selected texts has shown an increasing
concern (conscious or unconscious) with time in the later works.
Time has become more and more a part of the fabric of the plot
as it has become more and more externalized. With the development of time as part of the driving forces of the plot, it has
begun to sever its relation to the life-times of the individual.
There are no deadlines or time limits in the <u>Roland</u>, <u>Atlakviða</u>
or <u>Beowulf</u> although there is no narrative reason why there should
not be.   Later texts focus with increasing accuracy and
intensity on time as an organizing principle, and punctuality
assumes greater and greater significance. In <u>Gunnlaugs</u> <u>Saga</u>
a period of three years is set for Gunnlaug's betrothal. At
the Althing, after the third winter, Hrafn is told that Gunnlaug may still arrive before the end of the summer. The following year Helga is promised to Hrafn unless Gunnlaug arrives
before the "winter nights" in October. Even allowing for the
delicate family relationships, this is an extreme of temporal
flexibility; Gunnlaug was originally given three years but
this is extended to almost four and a half years.

Yvain exceeds his time limit of one year by six weeks and
has to undergoe his series of adventures to expiate his fault.
He becomes aware of time to such an extent that he comes to be
concerned about a single hour -- he must get back to Lunete
before mid-day which, even in those days when hours were variable, was always a <u>point</u> in time.

In <u>Sir</u> <u>Gawain</u> <u>and</u> <u>the</u> <u>Green</u> <u>Knight</u>, the hero is consistently concerned with being on time for his appointment with

the Green Knight and has to be persuaded by Sir Bertilak to
stay until the morning of the day set for his promised meeting.
Although no hour has been agreed upon, Gawain gets up before
daybreak after a sleepless night in order to make sure he will
be punctual, in spite of the fact that he has been assured
that the Green Chapel is less than two miles from Sir Bertilak's
castle.

"The Shipman's Tale" does not concentrate on punctuality,
but there is a strong sense of the external pressure of objective time. The monk consults his time-piece and announces
the time of day; the wife, impatient to dine, knocks on her
husband's door; and the husband travels from one place to another borrowing and repaying money against time.

Atlakviða and Roland are set in an almost timeless world,
in which if time is mentioned, it is subjective, qualitative
and completely bound up with action. The events begin and continue until they are finished. Nor are there any temporal
boundaries in Atlamál, although there is a linear sense of time,
of the past being different from the present, which is lacking
in Atlakviða and the Roland.

In Beowulf time has a different significance from that
in the other texts. There is no emphasis on a period of time
within which a task has to be accomplished nor a day on which
a crisis is to occur, but there are repeated contrasts between
past, present and future events. This gives a feeling of the
inevitability and linearity of the passage of time which is
quite absent from the other early works.

Differences in the significance of time are paralled by differences in narrative structure. Generally, in the early texts the significance and emotional intensity of a passage is conveyed by repetition and by the structural arrangement, and the narratives are discontinuous. In the later texts, a different kind of emotion is stressed, an uncertainty and expectation which is produced by the use of time. A linear narrative follows linear time from the past through the present to the unknown future.

I hope to have shown in this investigation that an analysis of texts from the point of view of time and structure can be enlightening in a comparison of oral and written literature. Although the texts chosen are from a variety of cultures and periods, their similarities and differences cross those cultural boundaries. From the point of view of our discussion the texts closer to one end of the oral-written spectrum have more in common than texts which share the same language. With these few examples, of course, it is difficult to draw firm conclusions. Detailed analyses of several texts of the same genres must be made, as well as investigations of the problem of time in other traditional genres, such as folktales.

As students of the past, we must learn to examine our texts in some sense as anthropologists should regard cultures other than their own, that is, without using our cultural framework as a Procrustean bed into which the product of the other culture is forced. This is particularly difficult -- and important -- with such fundamental concepts as those of time. We have seen, through the study of these texts, how profound are some of the differences between non-literate and literate cultures. The literature of the fourteenth century matches more closely our intellectual background. With the invention of the mechanical striking clock and of the fixed hour of sixty minutes, the day becomes an intellectual construct instead of the perceptual sequence of light and darkness. From that period onward the day begins, not by the order of Nature, but by the will of Man.

NOTES

[1]Richard Glasser, Time in French Life and Thought, (tr.)
C. G. Pearson (Manchester: Manchester University Press, 1972).
Glasser discusses different attitudes toward time in French
literature, and documents the kinds of contrasts we have in-
vestigated. But he makes no connection between the different
concepts and the kinds of society to which they belong; he
views the chansons de gestes as the products of undeveloped
minds: "objective time was frequently distorted. ...The part
played by time in the life of man was unknown to the author
of the Chanson de Roland" (pp. 12-13).

LIST OF WORKS CONSULTED

A bibliography of Time, in English alone, would fill many pages. This selection includes those works which I thought might be useful to my particular investigation.

GENERAL STUDIES, including discussions of literacy, time measurement, anthropology, sociology, psychology, and history.

Bartlett, F. C. Psychology and Primitive Culture. New York: Macmillan, 1923.

_____. Remembering. Cambridge (England): The University Press, 1932.

Bauschatz, Paul C. The Well and the Tree: World and Time in Early Germanic Culture. Amherst: University of Massachusetts, 1982.

Bloch, Marc. Feudal Society. Tr. L. A. Manyon. Chicago: Chicago University Press, 1964.

Bohannan, Laura. "A Geneaological Charter." Africa, 22 (1952), 301-352.

Bohannan, Paul. "Concepts of Time among the Tiv of Nigeria." Southwestern Journal of Anthropology, 9 (1953), 251-262.

Bruner, Jerome S. Studies in Cognitive Growth. New York: Wiley, 1966.

Butler, Edward Cuthbert. Benedictine Monachism. London: Longmaus, 1919.

Carothers, J. C. "Culture, Psychology, and the Written Word." Psychiatry, 22, 15-28.

Chaytor, H. L. From Script to Print. Cambridge (England): W. Heffer and Sons, 1945.

Chenu, M. D. Nature, Man, and Society in the Twelfth Century. Oxford: Clarendon, 1962.

Curshmann, Michael. "Oral Poetry in Medieval English, French, and German Literature: Some Notes on Recent Research." Speculum, 43 (1967), 36-52.

Doob, Leonard W. Patterning of Time. New Haven: Yale University Press, 1971.

Durkheim, Émile and Marcel Mauss. "De quelques formes primitives de Classification." L'Année Sociologique, 7 (1902-03), 1-72.

Durkheim, Émile. The Elementary Forms of the Religious Life.
Tr. J. W. Swain. New York: Macmillan, 1915.

_____. The Division of Labor in Society. Tr. G. Simpson.
Glencoe, Illinois: Free Press, 1947.

Eisenstein, Elizabeth L. "Some conjectures about the impact
of printing upon Western society and thought." Journal
of Modern History, 40 (1968), 1-56.

Einstein, Albert. "Space-Time." Encyclopedia Brittanica.
Chicago: Encyclopedia Brittanica, 1973. Vol. 20, 1070.

Eliade, Mircea. The Sacred and the Profane. Tr. Willard
Trask. New York: Harcourt Brace, 1959.

Evans-Pritchard, E. E. The Nuer. Oxford: Clarendon, 1940.

_____. Witchcraft, Oracles, and Magic among the Azande.
Clarendon, 1937.

Fischer, R. "Interdisciplinary perspectives of time." Annals
of the New York Academy of Sciences, 138 (1967), 367-915.

Fraisse, Paul. The Psychology of Time. Tr. Jennifer Leith.
London: Eyre and Spotiswoode, 1953.

_____. "Time: psychological aspects." The International
Encyclopedia of the Social Sciences. Eds. E.R.A.
Seligman and A. Johnson. New York: Macmillan, 1968.
Vol. 16, 25-30.

Fraser, J. T. The Voices of Time. New York: Braziller, 1965.

_____. The Study of Time. Proceedings of the International
Society for the Study of Time. New York: Braziller,
1972.

Gluckman, Max. "Social Beliefs and Individual Thinking in
Primitive Society." Memoirs and Proceedings of the
Manchester Literary and Philosophical Society, 91 (1949).

Goody, Jack and Ian Watts, eds. Literacy and Traditional
Societies. Cambridge (England): The University Press,
1963.

Gougenheim, G. "Recherches sur le fréquence et la disponibil-
ité." Colloque de Strasbourg 1964, Statistique et
Analyse Linguistique. Paris: Presses Universitaires de
France, 1966, 57-66.

Gumbrecht, Hans Ulrich. Funktionswandel und Rezeption.
Studien zur Hyperbole in Literarischen Texten de roman-
ishen Mittelalters. München: Wilhelm Fink Verlag, 1972.

Gurvitch, Georges. "Structure sociales et multiplicité des temps Bulletin de la Société de Philosophie Françaises, 52 (1958).

Guyau, J. M. La genèse de l'idée de temps. Paris: Alcan, 1890.

Hadingham, Evan. Circles and Standing Stones. New York: Doubleday, 1976.

Halbwachs, Maurice. Les Cadres Sociaux de la Mémoire. Paris: Alcan, 1925.

Hall, Edward T. The Silent Language. Garden City: Doubleday, 1959.

Hallowell, A. Irving. "Temporal Orientation in Western Civilization and in a Pre-literate Society." American Anthropologist, 39 (1937), no. 4.

Haskins, C. H. The Renaissance of the 12th Century. Cambridge (Mass.): Harvard University Press, 1939.

Hawkins, Gerald. Stonehenge Decoded. London: Fontana, 1970.

Janet, P. L'évolution de la mémoire et de la notation de temps. Paris: Chahine, 1928.

Knowles, Dom David. The Monastic Order in England. Cambridge (England): The University Press, 1950.

Leach, E. R. "Primitive Time-Reckoning." A History of Technology. Eds. C. J. Singer, E. J. Holmyard, and A. R. Hall. Oxford: Clarendon, 1958.

_____. "Symbolic Representation in Time." Rethinking Anthropology. The London School of Economics Monographs on Social Anthropology, no. 22. London: Athlone Press, 1966.

_____. "Time and False Noses." Explorations, 5 (June 1955), 30-35.

Lee, Dorothy D. "Codifications of Reality: Lineal and Non-Lineal." Freedom and Culture. Englewood Cliffs, N.J.: Prentice Hall, 1959.

Le Shan, Lawrence L. "Time Orientation and Social Class." Journal of Abnormal and Social Psychology, 37 (1952).

Lévi-Strauss, Claude. The Savage Mind. Chicago: Chicago University Press, 1966.

Marshack, Alexander. The Roots of Civilization. New York: McGraw Hill, 1972.

McLuhan, Marshall. The Gutenburg Galaxy. Toronto: University of Toronto Press, 1962.

Mead, Margaret, ed. Cultural Patterns and Technical Change. Paris: UNESCO, 1953.

Meyerhoff, Hans. Time in Literature. Berkeley and Los Angeles: University of California Press, 1955.

Miller, Johathan. McLuhan. London: Fontana, 1971.

Moore, Wilbert E. Man, Time, and Society. New York: Wiley, 1963.

Mumford, Lewis. Technics and Civilization. New York: Harcourt Brace, 1934.

Needham, Joseph. Time and Eastern Man. London: Royal Anthropological Institute of Great Britain and Northern Ireland, 1965.

Nicolaisen, W. F. H. "Time in Folk-Narrative" in Newal, Venetia J., ed. & introd., Folklore Studies in the Twentieth Century. Woodbridge, UK; Totowa, N.J.: Brewer; Rowman & Littlefield, 1980.

Nilsson, Martin P. Primitive Time-Reckoning. Tr. F. J. Fielden. Lund: C.W.K. Gleerup, 1920.

Ong, Walter J. The Presence of the Word. New Haven: Yale University Press, 1967.

_____. Rhetoric, Romance, and Technology. Ithaca: Cornell University Press, 1971.

Opie, Iona and Peter. Lore and Language of Schoolchildren. Oxford: Clarendon Press, 1959.

Ornstein, Robert E. On the Experience of Time. Harmondsworth: Penguin, 1975.

Patrides, C. A., ed. Aspects of Time. Manchester: Manchester University Press, 1976.

Piaget, Jean. The Child's Concept of Time. New York: Ballantine, 1968.

Pirenne, Henri. Economic and Social History of Medieval Europe. New York: Harcourt Brace, 1937.

Poulet, Georges. Studies in Human Time. Tr. Elliott Coleman. Baltimore: The Johns Hopkins Press, 1956.

Price-Williams, D. R. Cross Cultural Studies. Harmondsworth: Penguin, 1969.

Reisman, David. "The Oral and Written Traditions." Explorations, 6 (1956), 22-28.

Rothwell, W. "The Hours of the Day in Medieval French." French Studies, 13 (1959), 240-251.

Sayles, G. O. The Medieval Foundations of England. London: Methuen, University Paperbacks, 1966.

Southern, R. W. The Making of the Middle Ages. New Haven: Yale University Press, 1953.

Scholes, R. and R. Kellogg. The Nature of Narrative. New York: Oxford University Press, 1966.

Simpson, Jacqueline. Everyday Life in the Viking Age. London: Carousel, 1971.

Spengler, Oswald. The Decline of the West. Tr. C. F. Atkinson. New York: Knopf, 1934.

Tawney, R. H. Religion and the Rise of Capitalism. New York: Harcourt Brace, 1936.

de Thaon, Philippe. Li Cumpoz Philippe de Thaon. Ed. Eduard Mall. Strassburg, 1873.

Thornton, H. and A. Time and Style. London: Metheun, 1962.

Toulmin, Stephen and June Goodfield. The Discovery of Time. Harmondsworth: Penguin, 1967.

Tuve, Rosemond. Allegorical Images and Some Medieval Books and Their Posterity. Princeton, N.J.: Princeton University Press, 1966.

Van Genep, Arnold. The Rites of Passage. Tr. Monika B. Vizedom and Gabrielle L. Caffee. Chicago: Chicago University Press, 1960.

Vansina, Jan. Oral Tradition: A Study in Historical Methodology. Tr. H. M. Wright. Chicago: Aldine Press, 1965.

Ventris, Michael and John Chadwick. The Decipherment of Linear B. Cambridge (England): The University Press, 1958.

Vernon, Jack. Inside the Black Room. Harmondsworth: Penguin, 1966.

Ward, F. A. B. Handbook of the Collections Illustrating Time Measurement. Part I (1947) Historical Review; Part II (1955) Descriptive Catalogue. Science Museum, London: H.M. Stationary Office.

Weber, Max. From Max Weber: Essays in Sociology. Tr. H. H. Gerth and C. Wright Mills. New York: Oxford University Press, 1946.

White, Lynn Jr. Medieval Technology and Social Change. Oxford: Clarendon, 1962.

Whorf, Benjamin Lee. Language, Thought, and Reality. Cambridge (Mass.): Massachusetts Institute of Technology Press, 1956.

Wolff, P. "Le temps et sa mesure au Moyen Age." Annales E. S. C., 13 (1962), 1141-1145.

GENERAL LITERARY STUDIES

Abrahams, Roger D. "Creativity, Individuality, and the Traditional Singer." Studies in the Literary Imagination, 3 (1970), 5-34.

Auerbach, Erich. Mimesis. Tr. W. R. Trask. Princeton, N.J.: Princeton University Press, 1968.

Bassett, S. E. The Poetry of Homer. Berkeley and Los Angeles: University of California Press, 1938. Sather Classical Lectures, Vol. 15.

Bekker-Nielsen, Hans, Peter Foote, Andreas Haarder and Prebend Meulengracht Sørensen, eds. Medieval Narrative: A Symposium. Odense: Odense University Press, 1979.

Bergson, Henri. Essai sur les Données immediates de la Conscience. Paris: Alcan: 1920.

Bowra, C. M. Heroic Poetry. London: Macmillan, 1952.

Cassirer, E. The Philosophy of Symbolic Forms. Tr. Ralph Manheim. New Haven: Yale University Press, 1955.

Chadwick, H. M. and N. K. The Growth of Literature. Cambridge (England): The University Press, 1932-40.

Chadwick, H. M. The Heroic Age. Cambridge (England): The University Press, 1912.

Crosby, Ruth. "Oral Delivery in the Middle Ages." Speculum, 11 (1933), 88-100.

Curtius, E. R. European Literature and the Latin Middle Ages. Tr. W. R. Trask. New York: Harper and Row, 1953.

Dundes, Alan. "Oral Literature." Introduction to Cultural
    Anthropology. Ed. James A. Clifton. Boston: Houghton
    Miflin, 1968.

_____, ed. The Study of Folklore. Engelwood Cliffs, N.J.:
    Prentice Hall, 1964.

Foley, John Miles, ed. Oral Traditional Literature: A Fest-
    schrift for Albert Bates Lord. Columbus, Ohio: Slavica,
    1981.

Frye, Northrop. The Anatomy of Criticism: Four Essays. Prince-
    ton, N.J.: Princeton University Press, 1957.

Genette, Gerard. Narrative Discourse. Tr. Jane E. Lewis.
    Ithaca: Cornell University Press, 1980.

Grunmann-Gaudet, Minette and Robin F. Jones, eds. The Nature of
    Medieval Narrative. Lexington: French Forum, 1980.

Kellogg, Robert. "Oral Narrative, Written Books." Genre, 10
    (Winter 1977), 655-65.

Ker, W. P. Epic and Romance. London: Macmillan, 1908. New
    York: Dover, 1957.

Lord, A. B. The Singer of Tales. Cambridge (Mass.): Harvard
    University Press, 1960.

Notopoulos, James A. "Parataxis in Homer; a New Approach to
    Homeric Literary Criticsm." TAPA, 80 (1949), 1-23.

Ovitt, George Odell. Time as a Structural Element in Medieval
    Literature. Unpublished Ph.D. dissertation, Amherst:
    University of Massachusetts, 1979.

Parry, Milman. "The Distinctive Character of Enjambment in
    Homeric Verse." TAPA, 55 (1929), 200-220.

Rothwell, W., W. R. J. Barron, David Blamires and Lewis Thorpe,
    eds. Studies in Medieval Literature and Languages in
    Memory of Frederick Whitehead. Manchester: Manchester
    University Press, 1973.

Thompson, J. W. The Literacy of the Laity in the Middle Ages.
    Berkeley and Los Angeles: University of California Press,
    1939.

Vinaver, Eugene. The Rise of Romance. London: Oxford Uni-
    versity Press, 1971.

De Vries, Jan. Heroic Song and Heroic Legend. London: Oxford
    University Press, 1963.

ENGLISH

Bartlett, A. C. The Larger Rhetorical Patterns in Anglo-
Saxon Poetry. New York: Columbia University Press, 1935.

Baugh, Albert C. "Improvisation in the Middle English
Romances." Proceedings of the American Philosophical
Society, 103 (1959), 418-454.

Benson, Larry D. "The Literary Character of Anglo-Saxon Formü-
laic Verse." PMLA, 81 (1966), 334-341.

Bessinger, Jess B., ed. A Concordance to Beowulf. Ithaca:
Cornall University Press, 1969.

Bethurum, Dorothy, ed. Critical Approaches to Medieval
Literature. New York: Columbia University Press, 1960.

Blomfield, Joan. "The Style and Structure of Beowulf." The
Beowulf Poet. Ed. D. K. Fry. Englewood Cliffs, N.J.:
Prentice Hall, 1968.

Bloomfield, Morton W. "Sir Gawain and the Green Knight: An
Appraisal." PMLA, 76 (1961), 7-19.

Bonjour, Adrien. The Digressions in Beowulf. Oxford: Blackwells, 1950.

_____. "The Use of Anticipation in Beowulf." Review of English
Studies, 16 (1940), 291-299.

Borroff, Marie. Sir Gawain and the Green Knight: A Stylistic
and Metrical Study. New Haven: Yale University Press, 1962.

Brock, E. ed. and tr. "John of Hoveden's Practica Chilindri."
Essays on Chaucer, II, iii, no. 9. London: The Chaucer
Society, 1874.

Brodeur, A. G. The Art of Beowulf. Berkeley and Los Angeles:
University of California Press, 1959.

Bronson, Bertrand H. "Concerning 'Houres Twelve'." Modern
Language Notes, 58 (1953), 515-521.

Bryan, W. F. and Germaine Dempster. Sources and Analogues of
Chaucer's Canterbury Tales. New York: Humanities Press,
1958.

Burrow, J. A. A Reading of Sir Gawain and the Green Knight.
London: Routledge and Kegan Paul, 1965.

Campbell, A. P. "The Time Element of Interlace Structure in Beowulf." Neuphilologische Mitteilungen, 70 (1969), 425-435.

Fry, D. K. "Caedmon as a Formulaic Poet." Oral Literature: Seven Essays. Ed. J. J. Duggan. St. Andrews: Scottish Academic Press, 1975.

Irving, Edward B. Jr. Introduction to Beowulf. Englewood Cliffs, N.J.: Prentice Hall, 1969.

_____. A Reading of Beowulf. New Haven: Yale University Press, 1968.

Kottler, B. and A. M. Markham. A Concordance to Five Middle English Poems. Pittsburgh: Pittsburgh UP, 1966.

Leyerle, John. "The Interlace Structure of Beowulf." University of Toronto Quarterly, 37 (1967), 1-17.

Muscatine, Charles. Chaucer and the French Tradition. Berkeley and Los Angeles: University of California Press, 1957.

Nicholson, Lewis E. "The Art of Interlace in Beowulf." Studia Neophilogica, 52: 327-49.

Niles, John D. "Ring Composition and the Structure of Beowulf." PMLA, 94:924-35.

_____, ed. Old English Literature in Context: Ten Essays. Cambridge: Brewer; Totowa, N.J.: Rowman & Littlefield, 1980.

Nist, J. "The Structure of Beowulf." P.M.A.S.A.L., 43 (1958), 307-314.

Renoir, Alain. "Point of View and Design for Terror." The Beowulf Poet. Ed. D. K. Fry. Englewood Cliffs, N.J.: Prentice Hall, 1968.

Richardson, Janette. Blameth Nat Me. The Hague: Mouton, 1970.

Sisam, K. The Structure of Beowulf. London: Oxford University Press, 1967.

Spargo, J. W. "Chaucer's 'Shipman's Tale': The Lover's Gift Regained." Folklore Fellows Communication, no. 91. Helsinki, 1930.

Tolkien, J. R. R.   "Beowulf: The Monsters and the Critics."
     The Beowulf Poet.   Ed. D. K. Fry.   Englewood Cliffs, N.J.:
     Prentice Hall, 1968.

Utley, Francis Lee.   "Some Implications of Chaucer's Folktales."
     Laographia,   Athens, 1965.

Waldron, R. A.   "Oral-Formulaic Technique and Middle English
     Alliterative Poetry."   Speculum, 33 (1957), 79 2-804.

Wright, Herbert G.   "Good and Evil; Light and Darkness; Joy
     and Sorrow in Beowulf."   Review of English Studies (n.s.),
     8 (1957), 1-11.

FRENCH

Aebischer, Paul.   Rolandiana et Oliveriana.   Geneva: Droz, 1966.

Bloch, R. Howard.   French Medieval Literature and Law.   Berkeley
     and Los Angeles: University of California Press,
     1977.

Boissonnade, P.   De Nouveau sur La Chanson de Roland.   Paris:
     Champion, 1923.

Bezzola, R. R.   Le sens de l'aventure et de l'amour chez
     Chrétien de Troyes.   Paris: La jeune parque, 1947.

Cohen, Gustave.   "Combats judiciaire chez Chrétien de Troyes."
     Annales de l'Université de Paris, no. 8 (1933), 510-527.

Dodwell, Charles R.   "The Bayeux Tapestry and French Secular
     Epic."   The Burlington Magazine, 108 (1966), 549-560.

Duggan, J. J.   A Concordance of the Chanson de Roland.   Columbus:
     Ohio State University Press, 1969.

_____.   The Song of Roland: Formulaic Style and Poetic Craft.
     Berkeley and Los Angeles: University of California Press,
     1973.

Farnham, Fern.   "Romanesque Design in the Chanson de Roland."
     Romance Philology, 18 (1964), 143-164.

Fotich, Tatiana.   The narrative tenses in Chrétien de Troyes,
     a study in syntax and stylistics.   Washington: The
     Catholic University of America, 1950.

Frappier, Jean. Chrétien de Troyes, L'homme et l'oeuvre. Paris: Connaissance des Lettres, 1957.

_____. Le roman breton, Yvain ou le chevalier au lion. Paris: Paris: Centre de documentation Universitaire, 1952.

le Gentil, Pierre. La Chanson de Roland. Paris: Hetier-Boivin, 1955.

le Goff, J. La Civilisation de l'Occident médiéval. Paris: 1964.

Hatcher, Anna Granville, "Tense Usage in the Roland." Studies in Philology, 33 (1942), 597-624.

Imbs, Paul. Les Propositions temporelles en ancien français. Strasbourg: Faculté des Lettres de l'Université de Strasbourg, 1956.

Ménard, Philippe. "Le Temps et la durée dans les romans de Chrétien de Troyes." Moyen Age, 73 (1967), 375-401.

Menéndez-Pidal, Ramón. La Chanson de Roland et la tradition épique des Francs. Tr. I.-M. Chizel. Paris: Picard, 1960.

Newstead, Helaine. "Narrative Techniques in Chrétien's Yvain." Romance Philology, 30 (1977), 431-41.

Paquette, Jean-Marcel. "Epopée et Roman: Continué ou Discontinué?" Etudes Literaires (April 1971), 9-34.

Rychner, Jean. La Chanson de geste: Essai sur l'art épique des jongleurs. Geneva: Droz, 1955.

Schenck, David P. "Vues sur le Temps et l'Espace chez Chrétien de Troyes." Oeuvres et Critiques, 5 (1980-81), 111-17.

Vance, Eugene. "Spatial Structure in the Chanson de Roland." Modern Language Notes, 82 (1967), 602-26.

OLD NORSE

Allen, Richard F. Fire and Iron: Critical Approaches to Njáls Saga. Pittsburg: University of Pittsburgh, 1971.

Andersson, Theodore M. The Icelandic Family Saga: An Analytic Reading. Cambridge (Mass.): Harvard University Press, 1967.

_____. The Problem of Icelandic Saga Origins. New Haven: Yale University Press, 1965.

_____. "Splitting the Saga." Scandinavian Studies, 47 (1975), 437-441.

_____. "The Textual Evidence for an Oral Family Saga." Arkiv för Nordisk Filologi, 81 (1966), 1-23.

Bouman, Arie C. Patterns in Old English and Old Icelandic Literature. Leyden: Universitaire Pers, 1962.

Clover, Carol. "Scene in Saga Composition." Arkiv för Nordisk Filologi, 89 (1974), 57-83.

Einarsson, Stefan. A History of Icelandic Literature. Baltimore: The Johns Hopkins Press, 1955.

Foote, P. G. "Some Account of the Present State of Saga Research." Scandinavica, 4 (1965), 115-126.

Hallberg, Peter. The Icelandic Saga. Tr. Paul Schach. Lincoln, Nebreska: University of Nebreska, 1962.

Harris, Joseph. "Genre and Narrative Structure in some Íslendinga Þættir." Scandinavian Studies, 44 (1972), 1-27.

_____. "Genre in the Saga Literature: a Squib." Scandinavian Studies, 47 (1975), 427-436.

Holtsmark, Anne. "Heroic Poetry and Legendary Sagas." Bibliography of Old Norse and Icelandic Studies (1965), 9-21.

Jones, Gwyn. Erik the Red and Other Icelandic Sagas. Tr. with an introduction. London: Oxford University Press, 1961.

_____. "History and Fiction in the Sagas of Icelanders." Saga Book of the Viking Society for Northern Research, 13 (1952-53), 285-306.

Leach, H. G. Angevin Britain and Scandinavia. Cambridge (Mass.): Harvard University Press, 1921.

Liestøl, Knut. The Origin of the Icelandic Family Sagas. Tr. A. G. Jayne. Cambridge (Mass.): Harvard University Press, 1930.

Lönnroth, Lars. "The Concept of Genre in Saga Literature," Scandinavian Studies, 47 (1975), 419-426.

_____. European Sources of Icelandic Saga-Writing. Stockholm: Stockholm University Press, 1965.

_____. Njáls Saga: A Critical Introduction. Berkeley and Los Angeles: University of California Press, 1976.

_____. "Structural Divisions in the Njála Manuscripts." Arkiv för Nordisk Filologi, 90 (1975), 49-79.

Magnusson, Magnus and Hermann Pálsson, eds. and trans. Laxdaela Saga. London: Penguin, 1959.

Nordal, Sigurdur. The Historical Element in the Icelandic Family Sagas. W. P. Ker Memorial Lecture. Glasgow: Jackson, Son, and Company, 1957.

Phillpotts, Bertha. Edda and Saga. London: Butterworth, 1931.

Scheps, Walter. "Historicity and Oral Narrative in Njáls Saga." Scandinavian Studies, 46 (1974), 120-34.

Schlauch, Margaret. Romance in Iceland. New York: American Scandinavian Foundation: 1934.

Springer, Otto. "The Style of the Icelandic Family Sagas." JEGP, 38 (1939), 107-138.

Sveinsson, Einar Ól. Dating the Icelandic Sagas. London: London: Viking Society for Borthern Research, 1958.

_____. "The Icelandic Sagas and the Period in which their Authors Lived." Acta Philologica Scandinavica, 12 (1937), 71-90.

Turville-Petre, E. O. G. The Origins of Icelandic Literature. Oxford: Clarendon, 1953.

_____. "Notes on the Intellectual History of the Icelander." History, 27 (1942), 111-123.

TEXTS

Beowulf. Ed. Fr. Klaeber. Boston: D. C. Heath, 1950.

Sir Gawain and the Green Knight. Ed. J. R. R. Tolkien and E. V. Gordon. 2nd ed. by Norman Davis. Oxford: Clarendon, 1968.

The Works of Geoffrey Chaucer. Ed. F. N. Robinson. Cambridge (Mass.): Riverside Press, 1961.

La Chanson de Roland. Ed. J. Bedier. Paris: H. Piazza, 1964.

Les Romans de Chrétien de Troyes: IV: Le Chevalier Au Lion
    (Yvain). Ed. Mario Roques. Paris: Champion, 1974.

The Poetic Edda. Volume I: Heroic Poems. Ed. Ursula Dronke.
    London: Oxford University Press, 1969.

Gunnlaugs Saga Ormstungu. Eds. Sigurður Nordal and Guðni
    Jónsson. Íslenzk Fornrit, III Bindi, Borgfirðinga Sǫgur.
    Reykjavík: Hið Íslenzka Fornritafélag, 1938.

Corpus Codicum Islandicorum Medii Aevum, The Arnemagnaeæn
    Manuscript, 557, 4to. Copenhagen, Munksgaard, 1940.